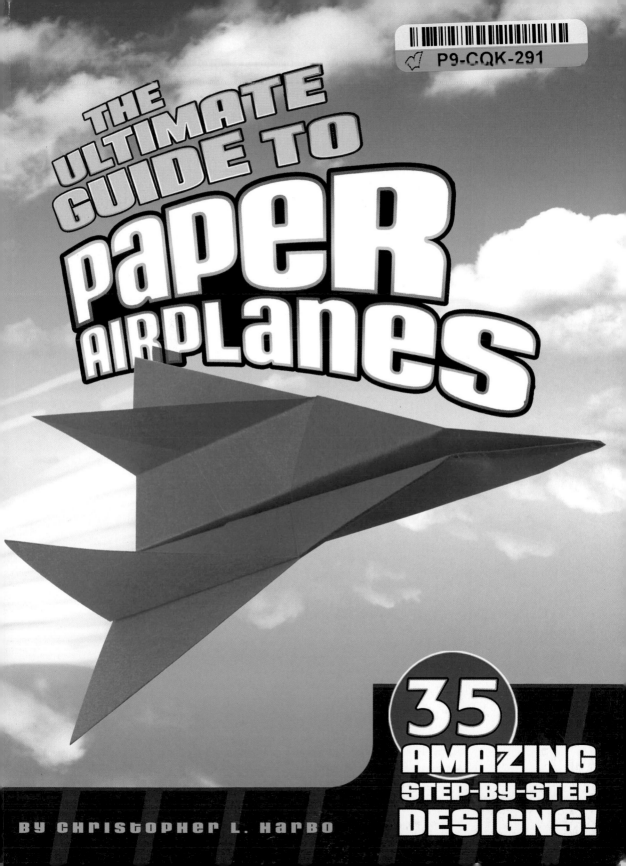

THE ULTIMATE GUIDE TO PAPER AIRPLANES

35 AMAZING STEP-BY-STEP DESIGNS!

BY CHRISTOPHER L. HARBO

TABLE OF

Materials 4

Techniques and Terms 6

Folding Symbols 7

Chapter 1 Flight School Level 1 8

Dynamic Dart 10

Spinning Blimp 12

Whirly 13

Helicopter 14

Flying Squirrel 16

Ring Wing 18

Tailspin 20

Long Ranger 22

V-Wing 24

Schoolyard Special 26

Elevator Glider 29

Long Shot Game 32

Chapter 2 Copilot Level 2 34

Air Shark 36

Wind Tunnel 38

Streaking Eagle 40

Parakeet 42

Whisper Dart 44

Vampire Bat 46

contents

ARROWHEAD 49

NIGHTHAWK 52

VAPOR 55

BULL'S-EYE GAME 58

CHAPTER 3 PILOT LEVEL 3 60

LIFTOFF 62

NEEDLE NOSE 64

AVIATOR 66

FANG 68

LAZY LANDER 71

HANG GLIDER 74

STEADY EDDIE 77

D-WING 80

HANG TIME GAME 84

CHAPTER 4 CAPTAIN LEVEL 4 86

FIGHTER JET 88

WARTHOG 91

GLIDING GRACE 94

FLYING ACCORDION 97

SPACE BOMBER 100

SPARROWHAWK 103

SCREECH OWL 106

AIRCRAFT CARRIER GAME 110

Materials

Every paper airplane builder needs a well-stocked toolbox. The models in this book use the materials listed below. Take a minute before you begin folding to gather what you need:

paper

Any paper you can fold will work. Notebook paper is always popular. But paper with cool colors and designs gives your planes style.

CLear TaPe

Most paper airplanes don't need tape. But when they do, you'll be glad you have it ready to go.

SCISSORS

Keep a scissors handy. Some models need a snip here or there to fly well.

RUBBER BANDS

Rubber bands can send some airplane models sailing. Long, thin rubber bands work well.

PAPER CLIPS

Paper clips are perfect for adding weight to a plane's nose. Have a supply of small and large paper clips on hand.

SMALL BINDER CLIPS

Small binder clips also give weight to a glider's nose.

Techniques and Terms

Folding paper airplanes isn't difficult when you understand common folding techniques and terms. Review this list before folding the models in this book. Remember to refer back to this list if you get stuck on a tricky step.

VALLEY FOLDS

Valley folds are represented by a dashed line. The paper is creased along the line. The top surface of the paper is folded against itself like a book.

Mountain FOLDS

Mountain folds are represented by a pink or white dashed and dotted line. The paper is creased along the line and folded behind.

Reverse FOLDS

Reverse folds are made by opening a pocket slightly and folding the model inside itself along existing creases.

Mark folds are light folds used to make reference creases for a later step. Ideally, a mark fold will not be seen in the finished model.

Rabbit ear folds are formed by bringing two edges of a point together using existing creases. The new point is folded to one side.

Squash folds are formed by lifting one edge of a pocket and reforming it so the spine gets flattened. The existing creases become new edges.

FOLDING SYMBOLS

Fold the paper in the direction of the arrow.

Fold the paper behind.

Fold the paper and then unfold it.

Turn the paper over or rotate it to a new position.

A fold or edge hidden under another layer of paper; also used to mark where to cut with a scissors

It's your first day of class, but your training schedule is packed. Eleven birds are waiting on the runway and you're itching to fly. Let's get started. It's time to earn your wings. Your first job is to flex those fingers. Paper gliders must be folded. But don't worry, the instructions won't strain your brain.

WELCOME TO FLIGHT SCHOOL!

These models are easy to fold. Just remember to follow the steps carefully and practice, practice, practice. Before you know it, your planes will fly all over the room.

Dynamic Dart 10

Spinning Blimp 12

Whirly 13

Helicopter 14

Flying Squirrel 16

Ring Wing 18

Tailspin 20

Long Ranger 22

V-Wing 24

Schoolyard Special 26

Elevator Glider 29

Dynamic Dart

TRADITIONAL MODEL

The Dynamic Dart is one of the most popular paper planes on the planet. It's the type of model that never lets you down. Best of all, its steps are super simple. You'll be folding it from memory in no time flat.

MATERIALS

* 8.5- by 11-inch (22- by 28-centimeter) paper

START HERE

1 Valley fold edge to edge and unfold.

2 Valley fold the corners to the center.

3 Valley fold the edges to the center.

10

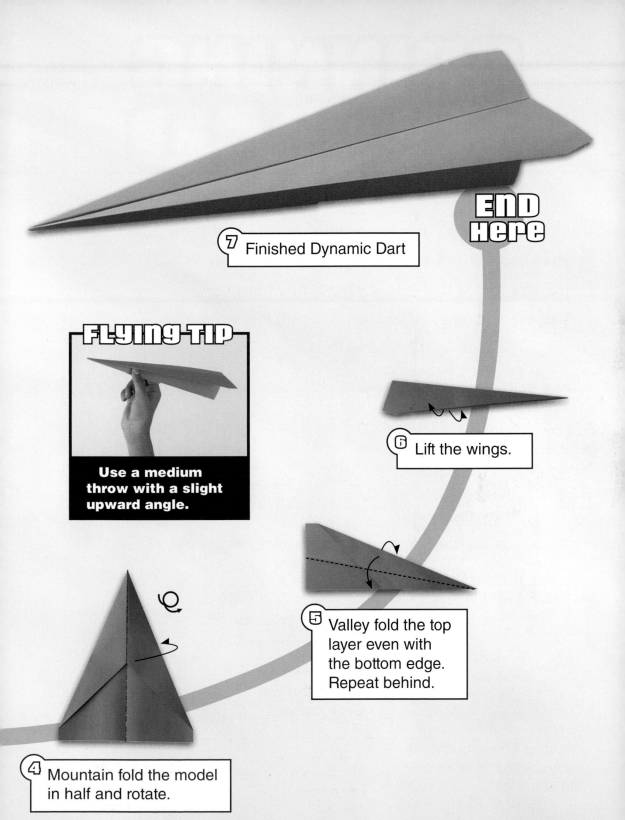

7 Finished Dynamic Dart

END HERE

FLYING TIP

Use a medium throw with a slight upward angle.

6 Lift the wings.

5 Valley fold the top layer even with the bottom edge. Repeat behind.

4 Mountain fold the model in half and rotate.

SPINNING BLIMP

TRADITIONAL MODEL

The Spinning Blimp is a clever paper toy. In your hand it looks like a ribbon. But in the air it spins so fast that it looks like a tiny blimp. Release it as high as you can and watch it twirl.

materials

* 8.5- by 11-inch (22- by 28-cm) paper
* scissors

END Here

5 Finished Spinning Blimp

4 Slide the slits together to form a loop.

Start Here

1 Cut a 1.25-inch (3-cm) strip off the paper's long side.

FLYING TIP

3 Bend the strip to bring the two slits together.

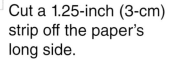

2 Cut slits about 2 inches (5 cm) from the ends of the strip. The slits should be on opposite sides of the strip.

Pinch one side of the model's loop with your index finger and thumb. Release with a gentle forward push.

WHIRLY

TRADITIONAL MODEL

How can a simple paper strip be so much fun? With two small folds, the Whirly looks like a useless scrap of paper. But launch it once and you'll want to watch it flutter to the floor over and over again.

MATERIALS

* 8.5- by 11-inch (22- by 28-cm) paper
* scissors

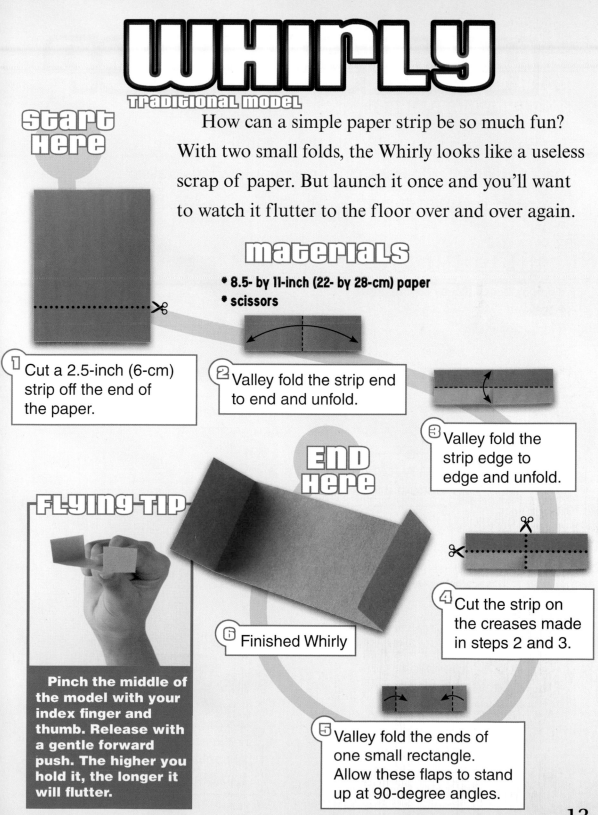

Start Here

1 Cut a 2.5-inch (6-cm) strip off the end of the paper.

2 Valley fold the strip end to end and unfold.

3 Valley fold the strip edge to edge and unfold.

4 Cut the strip on the creases made in steps 2 and 3.

5 Valley fold the ends of one small rectangle. Allow these flaps to stand up at 90-degree angles.

6 Finished Whirly

END HERE

FLYING TIP

Pinch the middle of the model with your index finger and thumb. Release with a gentle forward push. The higher you hold it, the longer it will flutter.

13

HELICOPTER

TRADITIONAL MODEL

With a snip here and a fold there, you'll make the paper Helicopter in less than three minutes. This classic toy never ceases to amaze. Go ahead, give it a whirl!

materials

* 8.5- by 11-inch (22- by 28-cm) paper
* scissors
* large paper clip

4 Valley fold the flaps.

5 Valley fold the bottom edge.

6 Add a paper clip to the folded edge.

7 Valley fold one propeller. Mountain fold the other propeller.

1 Cut a 3.5-inch (9-cm) strip off the paper's long side.

2 Cut a 5-inch (13-cm) slit down the center of the strip.

3 Cut two 1.25-inch (3-cm) slits in the sides of the strip. These slits should be about 4 inches (10 cm) from the bottom of the strip.

FLYING TIP

Pinch the paper clip with your index finger and thumb. Throw the model straight up into the air as high as you can. Watch it spin gracefully to the ground.

END Here

8 Finished Helicopter

FLYING SQUIRREL

TRADITIONAL MODEL

This glider is nothing more than a single wing. But gravity and air currents give it amazing flights. With the right push, the model will glide like a graceful flying squirrel.

MATERIALS

- 6-inch (15-cm) square of paper

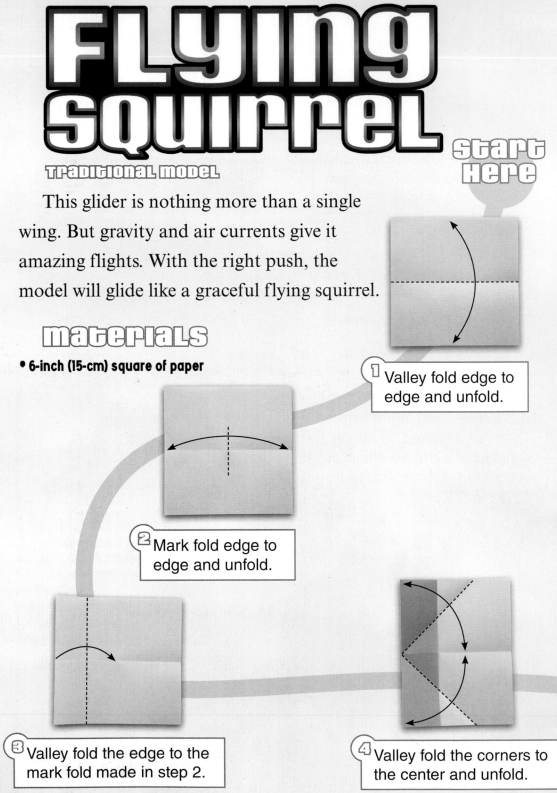

start Here

1 Valley fold edge to edge and unfold.

2 Mark fold edge to edge and unfold.

3 Valley fold the edge to the mark fold made in step 2.

4 Valley fold the corners to the center and unfold.

16

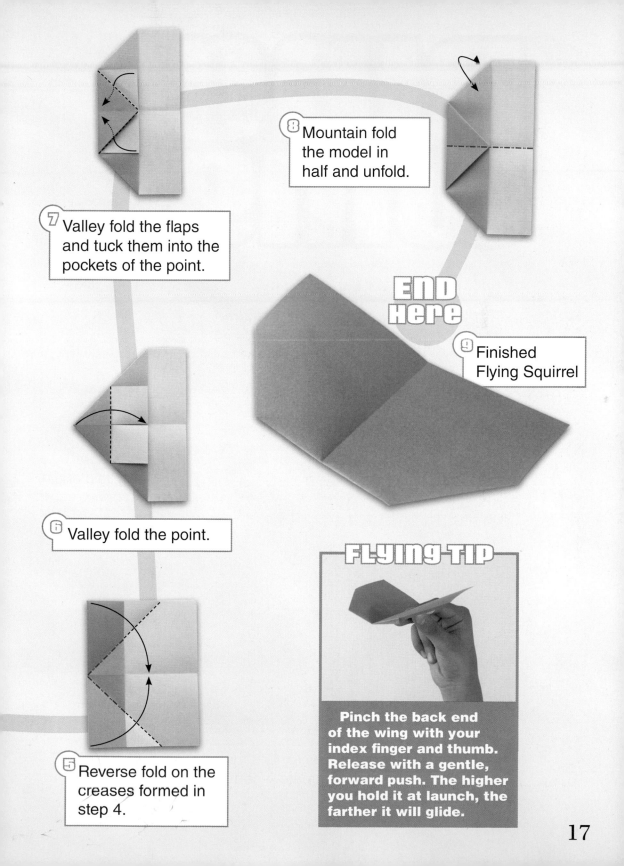

8 Mountain fold the model in half and unfold.

7 Valley fold the flaps and tuck them into the pockets of the point.

END Here

9 Finished Flying Squirrel

6 Valley fold the point.

FLYING TIP

Pinch the back end of the wing with your index finger and thumb. Release with a gentle, forward push. The higher you hold it at launch, the farther it will glide.

5 Reverse fold on the creases formed in step 4.

Ring Wing

The Ring Wing looks more like a napkin ring than a paper airplane. But this circular glider really sails.

materials

* 6-inch (15-cm) square of paper

Start Here

1 Valley fold point to point.

2 Valley fold the edge to create a narrow strip.

3 Valley fold again.

4 Bend the model to bring the ends of the strip together.

5 Tuck one end of the strip inside the other as far as it will go.

FLYING TIP

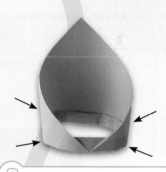

Hold the pointed end of the wing with your index finger and thumb. Release the Ring Wing with a gentle, forward push. Hold it high when you launch it to make it glide farther.

6 Shape the ring into a smooth circle.

7 Finished Ring Wing

END
Here

TAILSPIN

Some paper airplanes land smoothly. But the Tailspin prefers crash landings. With a hard throw, this model spins wildly through the air and crashes in a blaze of glory.

MATERIALS

* 8.5- by 11-inch (22- by 28-cm) paper

Start Here

1 Valley fold edge to edge and unfold.

2 Valley fold the corners to the center.

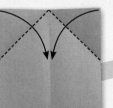

3 Valley fold the edges to the center.

4 Valley fold the point.

20

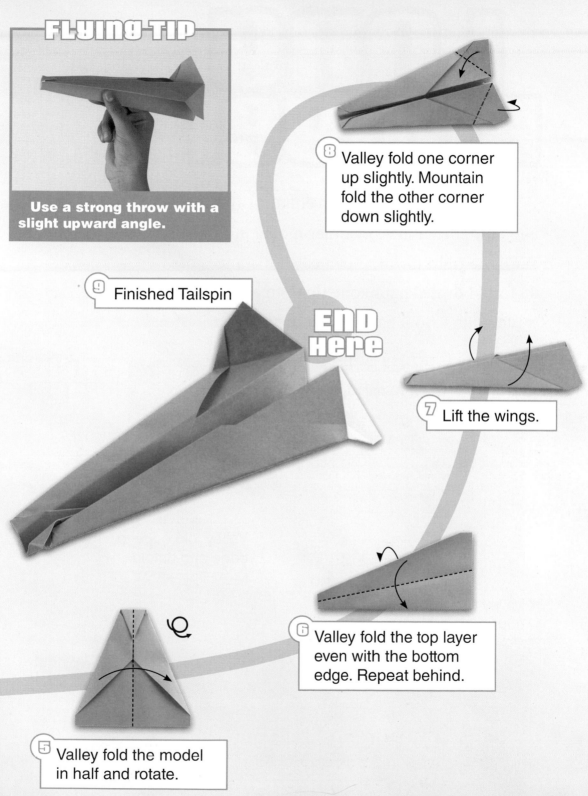

Use a strong throw with a slight upward angle.

8 Valley fold one corner up slightly. Mountain fold the other corner down slightly.

9 Finished Tailspin

END HERE

7 Lift the wings.

6 Valley fold the top layer even with the bottom edge. Repeat behind.

5 Valley fold the model in half and rotate.

Long Ranger

The Long Ranger has no equal. It flies farther and straighter than any other model in this book. With the right throw, it can cover distances of 45 feet (14 m). That's something to remember when your school has a paper airplane contest.

materials

* 8.5- by 11-inch (22- by 28-cm) paper

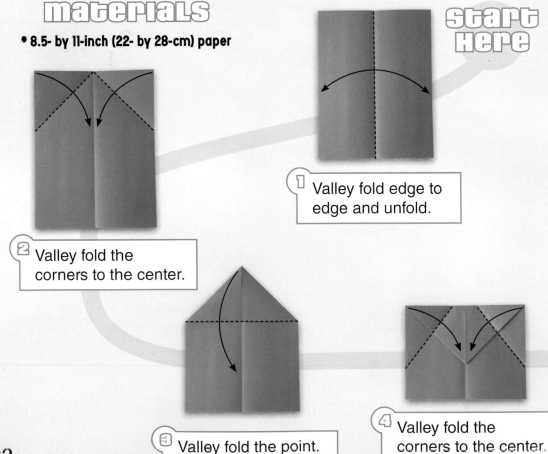

start Here

1. Valley fold edge to edge and unfold.

2. Valley fold the corners to the center.

3. Valley fold the point.

4. Valley fold the corners to the center.

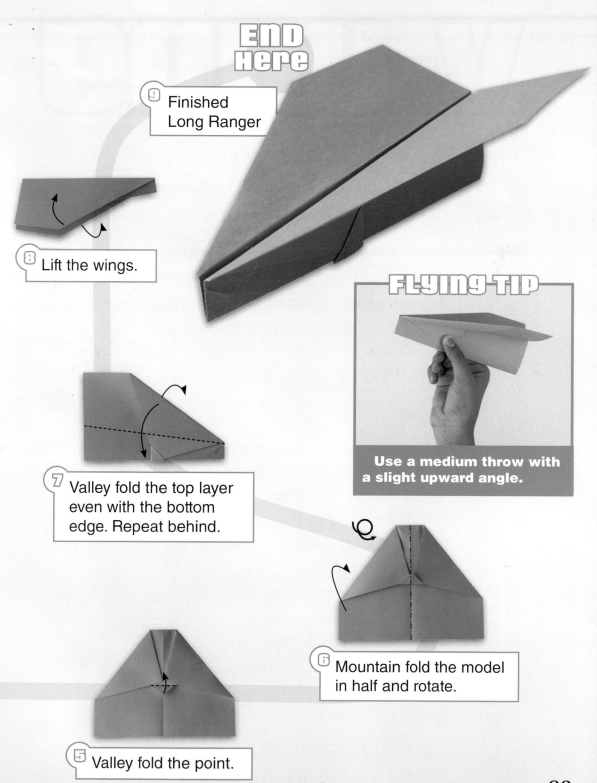

END Here

⑨ Finished Long Ranger

⑧ Lift the wings.

FLYING TIP

Use a medium throw with a slight upward angle.

⑦ Valley fold the top layer even with the bottom edge. Repeat behind.

⑥ Mountain fold the model in half and rotate.

⑤ Valley fold the point.

23

V-wing

If you need a spy plane, the V-wing is your ride. This glider combines a classic look with a very smooth flight. The plane seems to float on a cushion of air.

materials

* 10-inch (25-cm) square of paper

start Here

2 Valley fold the corners to the center.

1 Valley fold edge to edge and unfold.

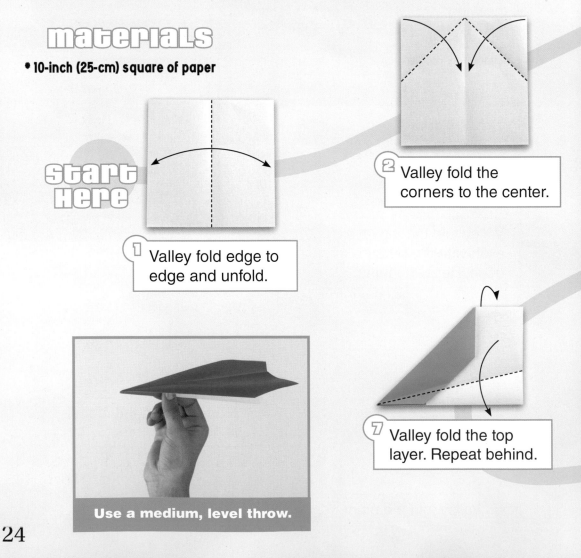

7 Valley fold the top layer. Repeat behind.

Use a medium, level throw.

24

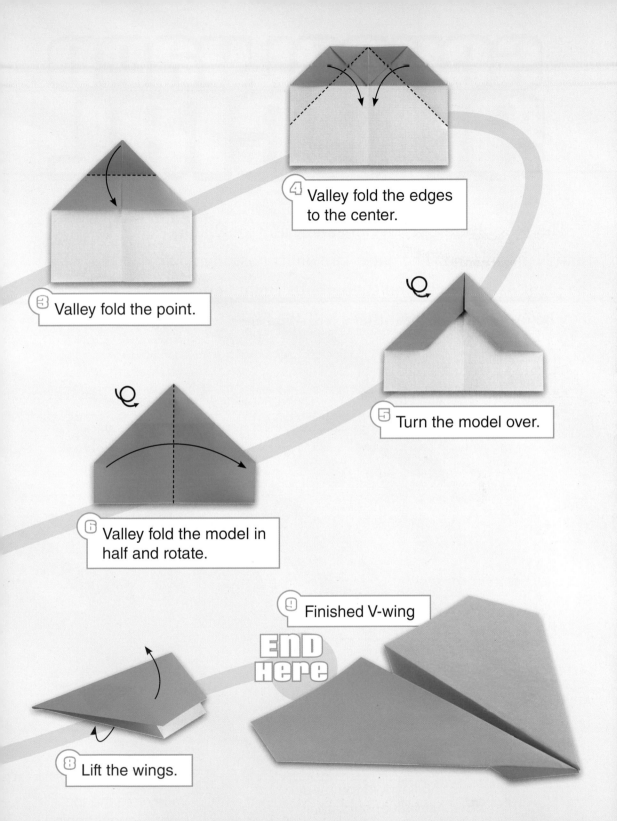

4 Valley fold the edges to the center.

3 Valley fold the point.

5 Turn the model over.

6 Valley fold the model in half and rotate.

9 Finished V-wing

END Here

8 Lift the wings.

SCHOOLYARD SPECIAL

TRADITIONAL MODEL

The Schoolyard Special can handle any rough and tumble playground. The paper clip on its nose gives the plane extra weight and strength. Its flight patterns may be unpredictable, but that's half the fun!

materials

* 8.5- by 11-inch (22- by 28-cm) paper
* small paper clip

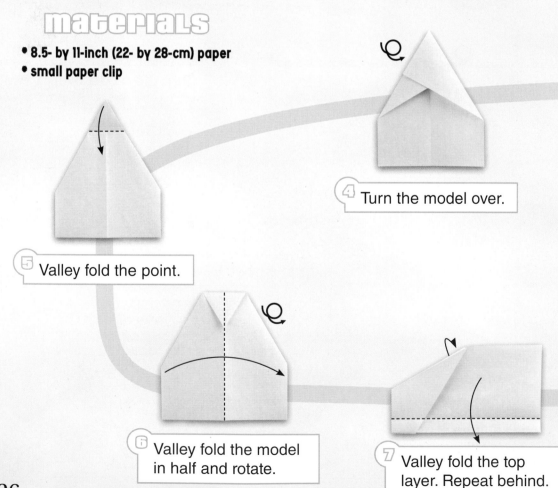

4 Turn the model over.

5 Valley fold the point.

6 Valley fold the model in half and rotate.

7 Valley fold the top layer. Repeat behind.

26

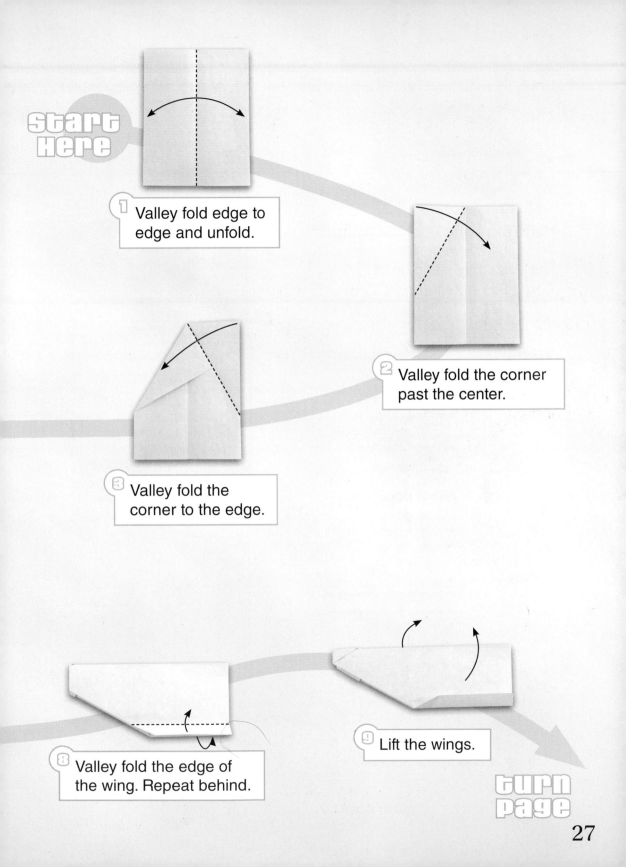

start
Here

1. Valley fold edge to edge and unfold.

2. Valley fold the corner past the center.

3. Valley fold the corner to the edge.

8. Valley fold the edge of the wing. Repeat behind.

9. Lift the wings.

turn
page

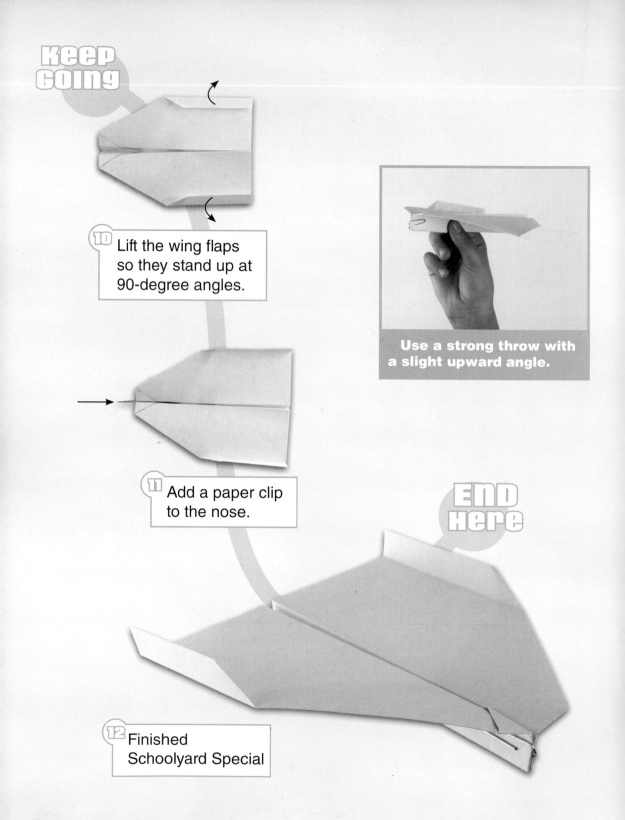

10 Lift the wing flaps so they stand up at 90-degree angles.

Use a strong throw with a slight upward angle.

11 Add a paper clip to the nose.

END HERE

12 Finished Schoolyard Special

Elevator GLIDER

TRADITIONAL MODEL

If you like to tinker with flight patterns, the Elevator Glider is just for you. It gets its name from the small elevator flaps on the wings. Adjust the angles of these flaps to find the flight that fits you right.

* 8.5- by 11-inch (22- by 28-cm) paper
* scissors

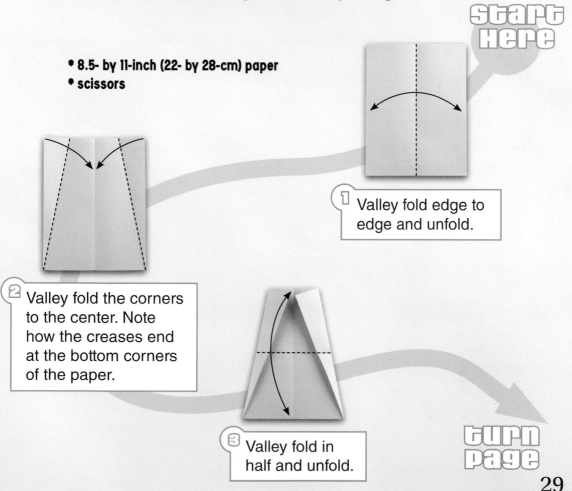

Start Here

1 Valley fold edge to edge and unfold.

2 Valley fold the corners to the center. Note how the creases end at the bottom corners of the paper.

3 Valley fold in half and unfold.

turn page

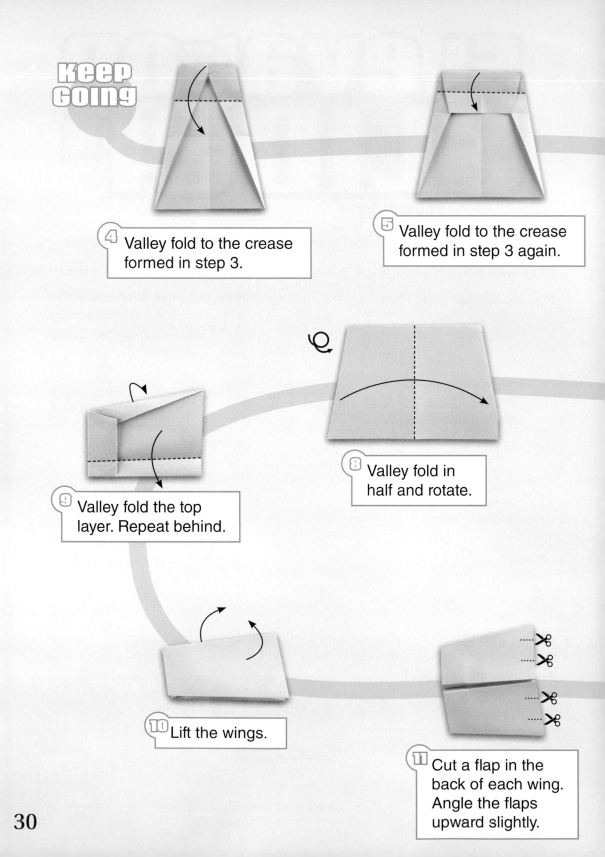

4 Valley fold to the crease formed in step 3.

5 Valley fold to the crease formed in step 3 again.

8 Valley fold in half and rotate.

9 Valley fold the top layer. Repeat behind.

10 Lift the wings.

11 Cut a flap in the back of each wing. Angle the flaps upward slightly.

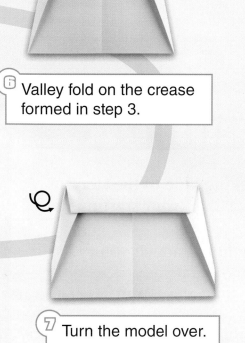

6 Valley fold on the crease formed in step 3.

Use a medium, level throw. Adjust the elevator flaps to control how the plane rises or dives.

7 Turn the model over.

END Here

12 Finished Elevator Glider

LONG SHOT

The best part of making paper airplanes is seeing how far they fly. Challenge a friend to a game of Long Shot.

materials
- masking tape
- large room
- 2 paper airplanes
- tape measure
- pencil
- notepad
- calculator

WHAT YOU DO

1. Stick a long piece of masking tape to the floor at one end of a large room. This is your starting line.

2. Stand behind the starting line. Launch your planes at the same time.

3. Measure the distance from the starting line to each plane. Write these measurements on a notepad beside your names.

4. Repeat steps 2 and 3 nine more times.

5. Use a calculator to add together the 10 measurements for one plane. Divide the total by the number 10. The answer you get will be the average distance the plane flew.

6. Repeat step 5 for the other plane.

7. Compare the two averages. The plane with the highest average wins the game.

CONGRATULATIONS!

Your flight training is complete. Now you're ready for the copilot seat. Grab another stack of paper and head straight to the next chapter. In Copilot Level 2, you'll learn the secrets to making the Air Shark, Whisper Dart, Nighthawk, and many other amazing planes. The skill level for these models gets kicked up a notch, but your training won't let you down.

JUMP RIGHT IN!
your next flight is just a few folds away!

You've passed flight school and earned your seat next to the pilot. Now it's time to get a feel for those flight controls. Nine airplanes need your help getting airborne.

WELCOME TO THE COCKPIT!

Your first task as copilot is to practice folding. Remember to make your folds cleanly and crisply. In no time your paper gliders will be soaring all over the neighborhood.

AIR SHARK • • • • • • • • • 36

WIND TUNNEL • • • • • • • • 38

STREAKING EAGLE • • • • • • • • • 40

PARAKEET • • • • • • • • 42

WHISPER DART • • • • • • • • • 44

VAMPIRE BAT • • • • • • • • • 46

ARROWHEAD • • • • • • • • 49

NIGHTHAWK • • • • • • • • 52

VAPOR • • • • • • • • 55

Air Shark

Traditional model

Prowl the skies with your very own Air Shark. This sturdy plane has a smooth, steady glide. It's a paper predator that's always ready to hunt.

materials

• 8.5- by 11-inch (22- by 28-centimeter) paper

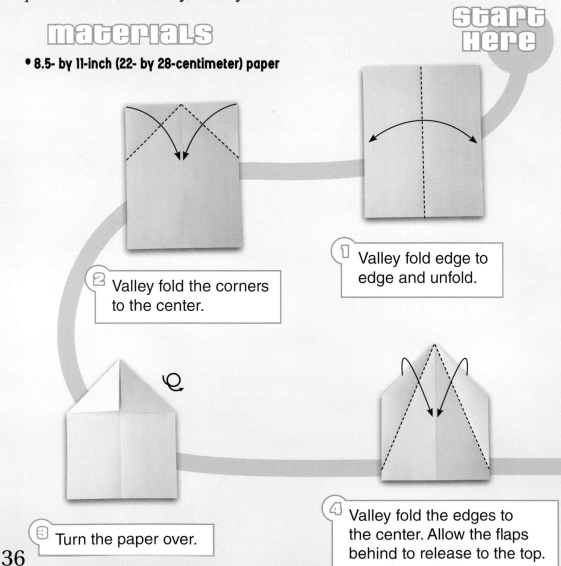

Start Here

1 Valley fold edge to edge and unfold.

2 Valley fold the corners to the center.

3 Turn the paper over.

4 Valley fold the edges to the center. Allow the flaps behind to release to the top.

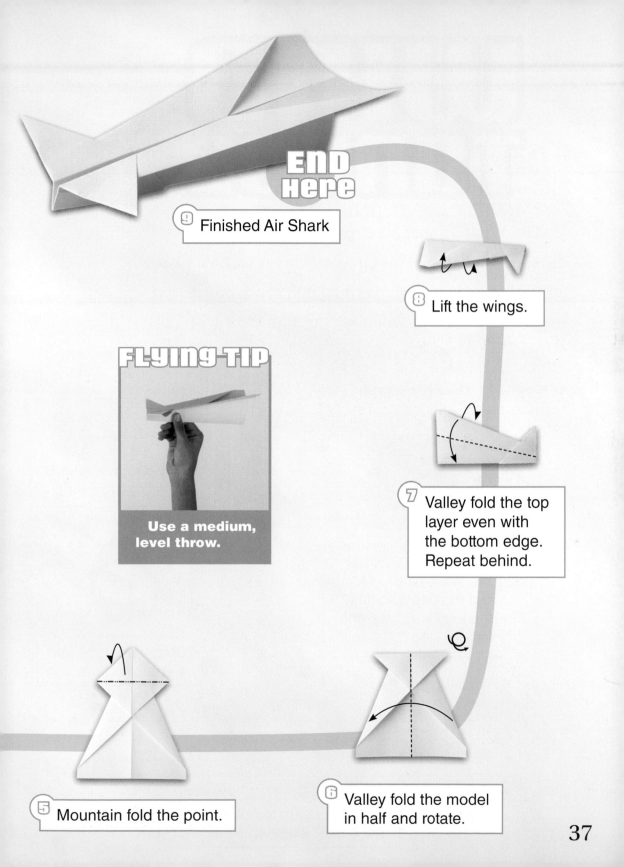

END HERE

⑨ Finished Air Shark

⑧ Lift the wings.

FLYING TIP

Use a medium, level throw.

⑦ Valley fold the top layer even with the bottom edge. Repeat behind.

⑤ Mountain fold the point.

⑥ Valley fold the model in half and rotate.

37

WIND Tunnel

TRADITIONAL MODEL

The Wind Tunnel takes paper airplanes in a very different direction. This circular wing is thrown like a football. Get your arm warmed up. You'll be amazed by how far this tube will glide through the air.

materials

* 8.5- by 11-inch (22- by 28-cm) paper
* scissors
* tape

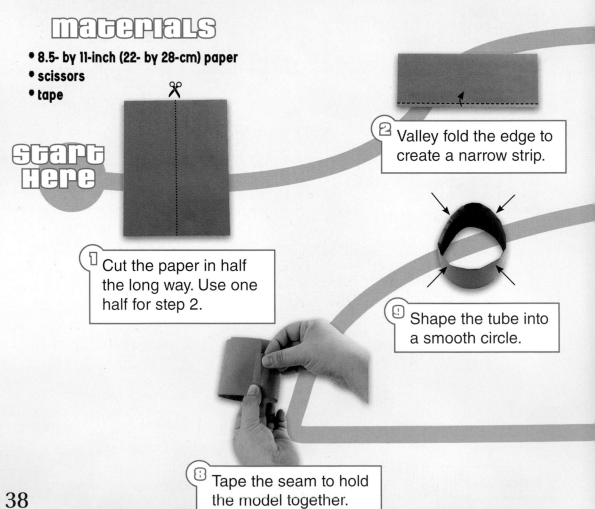

Start Here

1 Cut the paper in half the long way. Use one half for step 2.

2 Valley fold the edge to create a narrow strip.

9 Shape the tube into a smooth circle.

8 Tape the seam to hold the model together.

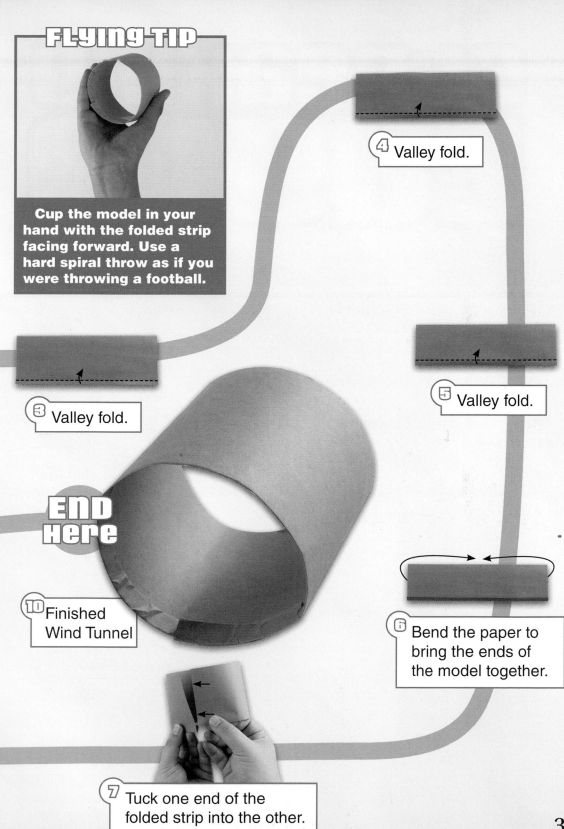

Cup the model in your hand with the folded strip facing forward. Use a hard spiral throw as if you were throwing a football.

4 Valley fold.

3 Valley fold.

5 Valley fold.

END HERE

10 Finished Wind Tunnel

6 Bend the paper to bring the ends of the model together.

7 Tuck one end of the folded strip into the other.

streaking Eagle

TRADITIONAL MODEL

The Streaking Eagle combines style and mechanics. Sleek wing flaps help the plane fly straight. Elevator flaps let you control how the plane rises or dives.

materials

* 8.5- by 11-inch (22- by 28-cm) paper
* scissors

9 Cut a flap in the back of each wing. Angle the flaps upward slightly.

END HERE

10 Finished Streaking Eagle

FLYING TIP

Use a medium, level throw. Adjust the elevator flaps to control the flight path.

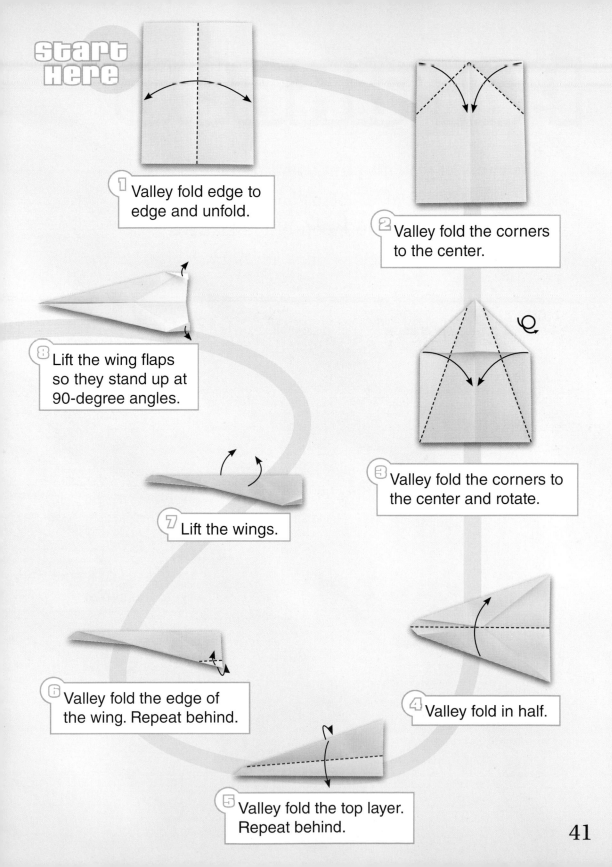

1. Valley fold edge to edge and unfold.

2. Valley fold the corners to the center.

3. Valley fold the corners to the center and rotate.

4. Valley fold in half.

5. Valley fold the top layer. Repeat behind.

6. Valley fold the edge of the wing. Repeat behind.

7. Lift the wings.

8. Lift the wing flaps so they stand up at 90-degree angles.

41

parakeet

The Parakeet is a little plane with a lot of attitude. This feisty model doesn't bother with a straight flight. It prefers to swoop, dive, and curve through the air. Each flight is a new adventure.

MATERIALS

* 6-inch (15-cm) square of paper

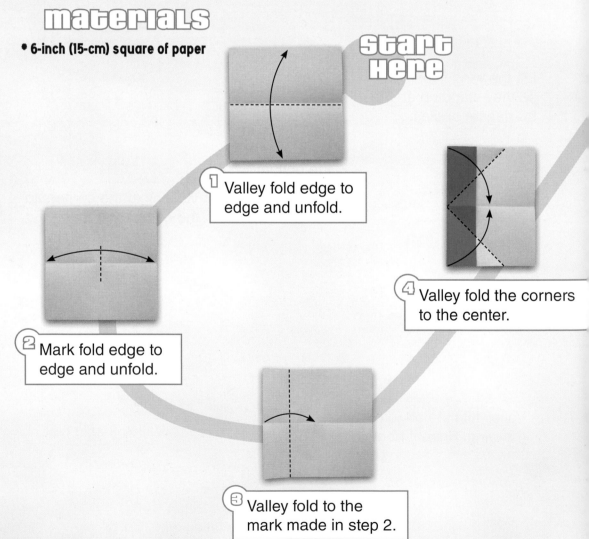

START HERE

1 Valley fold edge to edge and unfold.

2 Mark fold edge to edge and unfold.

3 Valley fold to the mark made in step 2.

4 Valley fold the corners to the center.

42

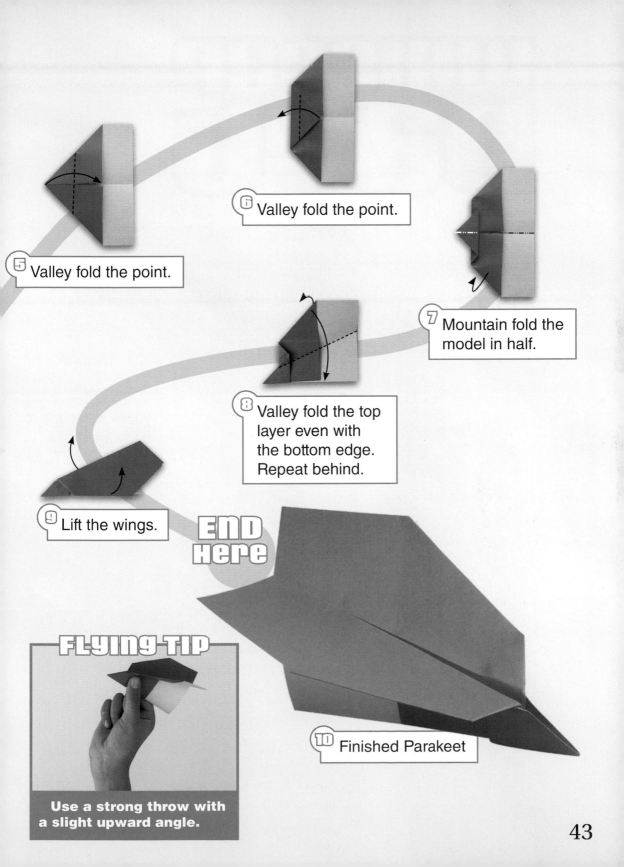

5 Valley fold the point.

6 Valley fold the point.

7 Mountain fold the model in half.

8 Valley fold the top layer even with the bottom edge. Repeat behind.

9 Lift the wings.

END HERE

10 Finished Parakeet

FLYING TIP

Use a strong throw with a slight upward angle.

WHISPER Dart

DESIGNED BY CHRISTOPHER L. HARBO

The Whisper Dart has a secret. It looks like a simple paper airplane. But a couple of extra folds give it added weight in the nose. Do you have your eye on a target across the room? This design will deliver!

materials

* 8.5- by 11-inch (22- by 28-cm) paper

Start Here

1 Valley fold edge to edge and unfold.

2 Valley fold the corners to the center. Note how the creases end at the bottom corners of the paper.

3 Valley fold to point A.

A

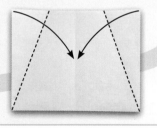

4 Valley fold.

44

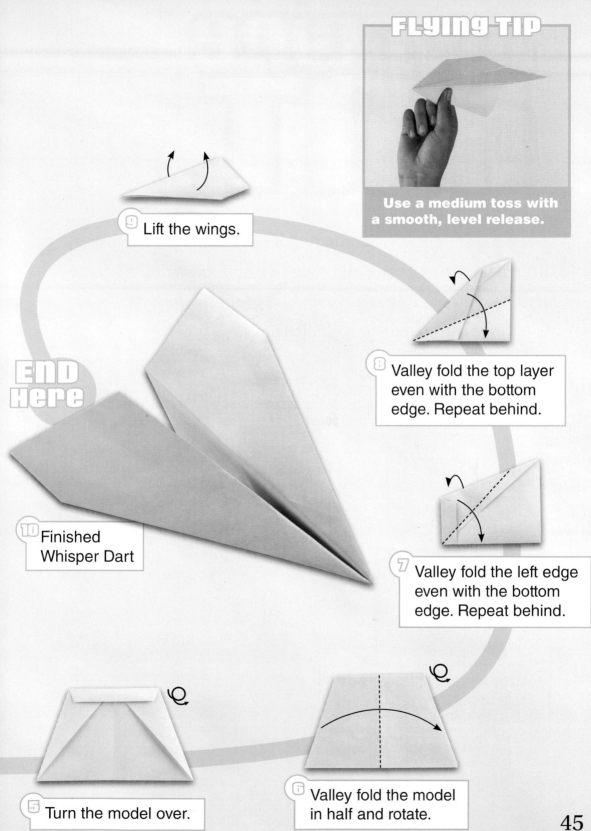

Use a medium toss with a smooth, level release.

9 Lift the wings.

8 Valley fold the top layer even with the bottom edge. Repeat behind.

END Here

10 Finished Whisper Dart

7 Valley fold the left edge even with the bottom edge. Repeat behind.

5 Turn the model over.

6 Valley fold the model in half and rotate.

45

vampire
BaT

Traditional model

The Vampire Bat's flight path is a jaw-dropper. This amazing wing soars and swoops when thrown correctly. Folding it is easy. Finding a room large enough to fly it in may be a challenge.

materials

* 8.5- by 11-inch (22- by 28-cm) paper

Start Here

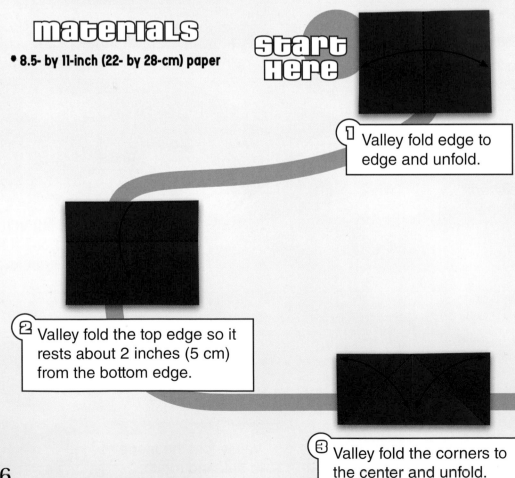

1 Valley fold edge to edge and unfold.

2 Valley fold the top edge so it rests about 2 inches (5 cm) from the bottom edge.

3 Valley fold the corners to the center and unfold.

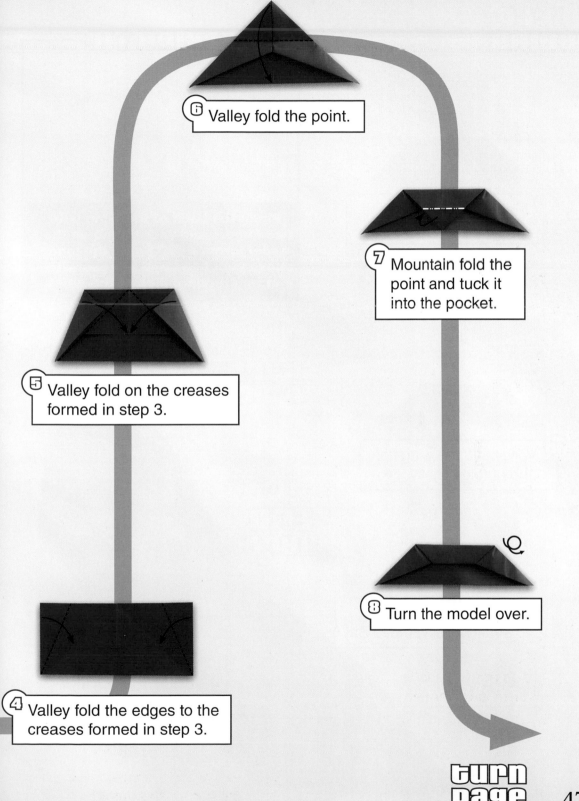

6 Valley fold the point.

7 Mountain fold the point and tuck it into the pocket.

5 Valley fold on the creases formed in step 3.

8 Turn the model over.

4 Valley fold the edges to the creases formed in step 3.

Pinch the back of the wing with two fingers and your thumb so the model forms a "V." Raise the model above your head and release with a strong forward flick of the wrist.

9 Mountain fold the wings and unfold slightly.

10 Valley fold the wing tips and unfold slightly.

END HERE

11 Finished Vampire Bat

ARROWHEAD

TRADITIONAL MODEL

Get ready to soar! The Arrowhead is a flying champion. This plane can cover amazing distances with very little effort. You'll get your exercise chasing this model from one end of the room to the other.

materials

* 8.5- by 11-inch (22- by 28-cm) paper

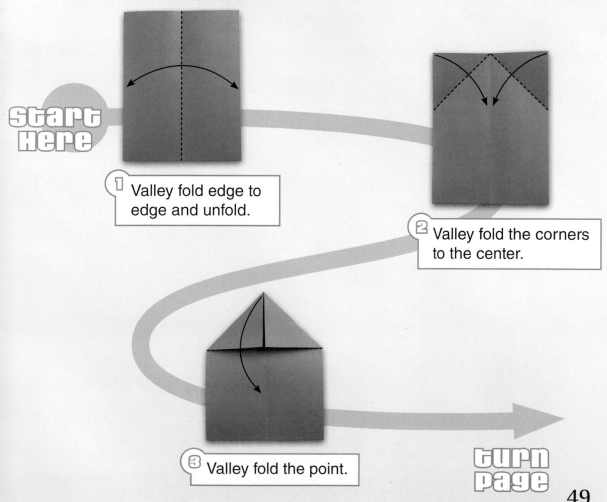

Start Here

1 Valley fold edge to edge and unfold.

2 Valley fold the corners to the center.

3 Valley fold the point.

turn page

49

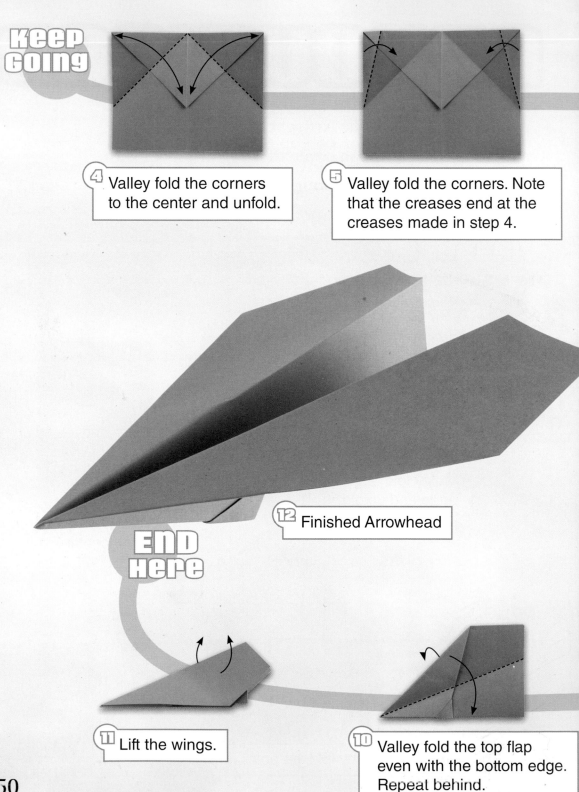

④ Valley fold the corners to the center and unfold.

⑤ Valley fold the corners. Note that the creases end at the creases made in step 4.

⑫ Finished Arrowhead

END HERE

⑪ Lift the wings.

⑩ Valley fold the top flap even with the bottom edge. Repeat behind.

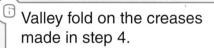

6 Valley fold on the creases made in step 4.

FLYING TIP

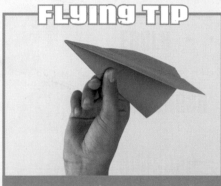

Use a medium throw with a slight upward angle.

7 Valley fold the point.

8 Turn the model over.

9 Valley fold the model in half and rotate.

NIGHTHAWK

The Nighthawk is a great flier with a simple design. This classic glider isn't fancy, but its graceful flight is sure to impress. Make two planes and challenge a friend to a flight contest.

materials

* 8.5- by 11-inch (22- by 28-cm) paper

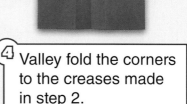

4 Valley fold the corners to the creases made in step 2.

5 Valley fold the point.

6 Valley fold the corners to the center crease.

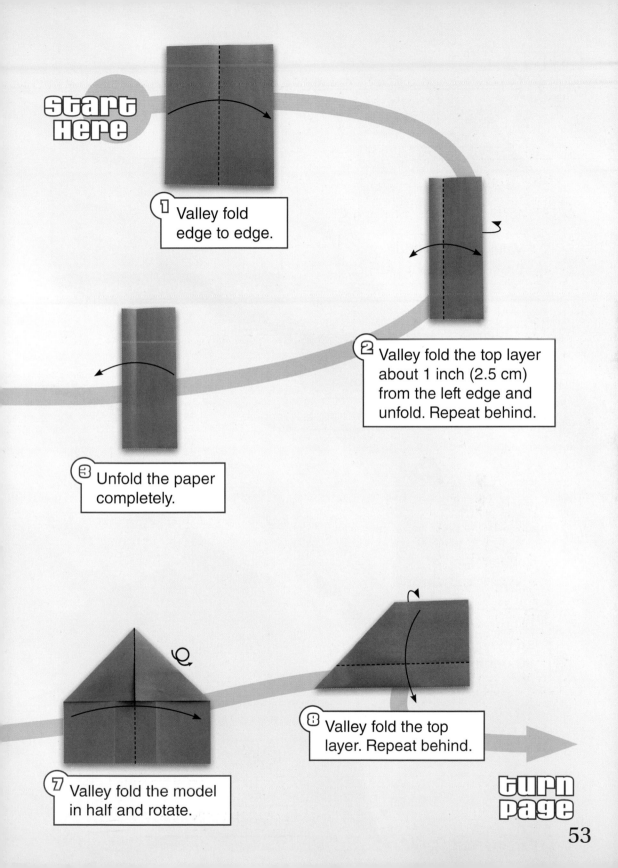

Start Here

1 Valley fold edge to edge.

2 Valley fold the top layer about 1 inch (2.5 cm) from the left edge and unfold. Repeat behind.

3 Unfold the paper completely.

7 Valley fold the model in half and rotate.

8 Valley fold the top layer. Repeat behind.

turn page

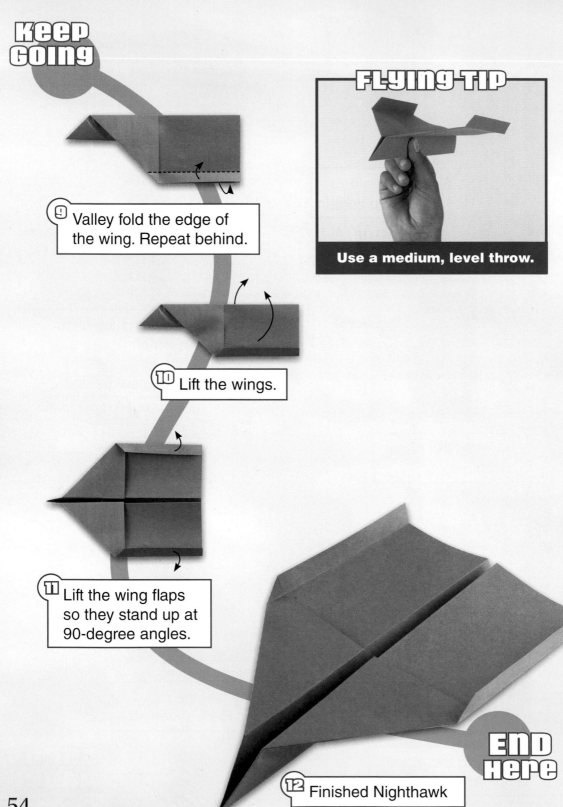

FLYING TIP

Use a medium, level throw.

⑨ Valley fold the edge of the wing. Repeat behind.

⑩ Lift the wings.

⑪ Lift the wing flaps so they stand up at 90-degree angles.

⑫ Finished Nighthawk

END HERE

54

Vapor

DESIGNED BY CHRISTOPHER L. HARBO

The Vapor has extra folds in the nose for strength and balance. The wing flaps guide the plane on an even flight. With very little effort, this model will slip silently from your hand and arc across the room.

MATERIALS

* 8.5- by 11-inch (22- by 28-cm) paper

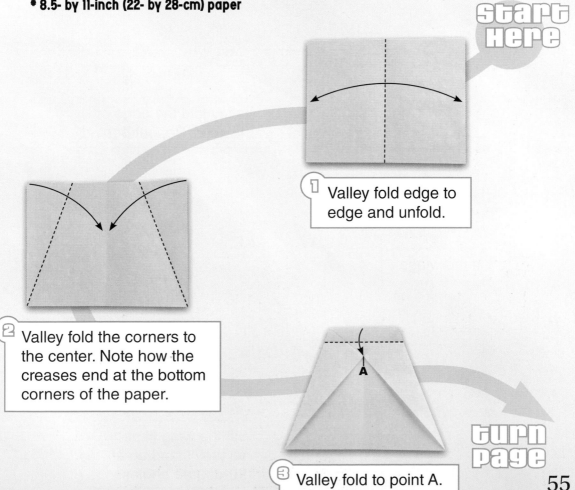

start here

1 Valley fold edge to edge and unfold.

2 Valley fold the corners to the center. Note how the creases end at the bottom corners of the paper.

3 Valley fold to point A.

A

turn page

55

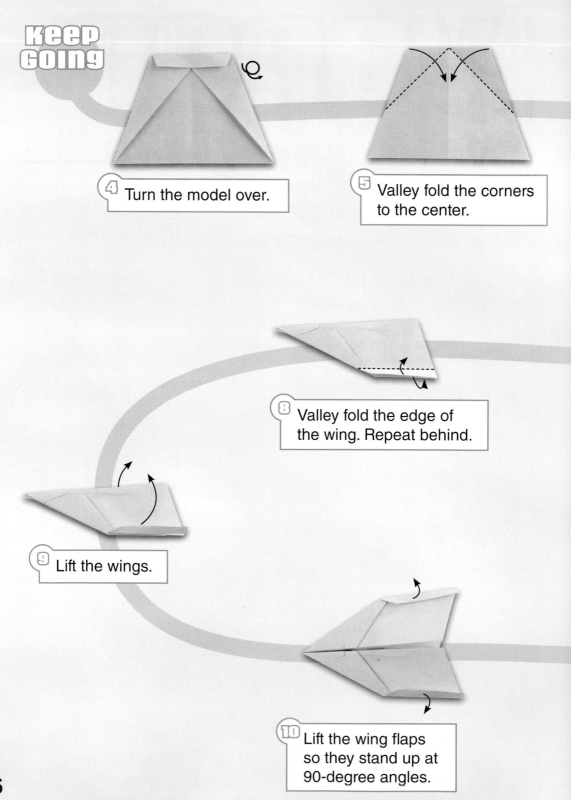

4 Turn the model over.

5 Valley fold the corners to the center.

8 Valley fold the edge of the wing. Repeat behind.

9 Lift the wings.

10 Lift the wing flaps so they stand up at 90-degree angles.

6 Valley fold the model in half and rotate.

FLYING TIP

Use a medium, smooth throw with a slight upward angle.

7 Valley fold the top layer. Repeat behind.

END Here

11 Finished Vapor

57

BULL'S-EYE

How accurate is your aim? Find out by challenging a friend to a game of Bull's-eye!

materials

- twine
- hula hoop
- masking tape
- 2 paper airplanes
- pencil
- notepad

WHAT YOU DO

1. Tie one end of a piece of twine to a hula hoop.

2. Tape the other end of the twine to the top of an open door frame. Allow the hoop to hang about 4 feet (1.2 meters) off the ground. If the hoop is too large for the doorway, simply allow it to straddle the door frame.

3. Walk 15 to 20 steps away from the hoop and turn around. Mark this spot on the floor with a piece of tape. The tape marks your throwing line.

4. Take turns throwing your paper airplanes from the throwing line. Planes that fly through the hoop score 5 points. Planes that fly above or below the hoop and through the doorway score 3 points. Planes that fail to pass through the hoop or the doorway receive no points.

5. Write down your scores on the notepad after each throw. After each player throws 10 times, add up the scores. The player with the highest score is the Bull's-eye champion!

WELL DONE, COPILOT!

Your practice has paid off. Now you're ready to move up the ranks in the next chapter. In Pilot Level 3, your fingers will fold their way through the Needle Nose, Fang, Lazy Lander, and many other dynamic planes. These models have more steps and trickier folds, but at this point you have no fear of flying.

get ready
to send a whole new sqadron of planes soaring through the air.

You've earned the rank of pilot and
you're ready to fly. Now it's time to prepare
eight planes for takeoff. Are you up to the
challenge? Strap yourself into the pilot's seat
and let's find out. As pilot, your first duty is
to polish your paper folding skills.

WELCOME ABOARD!

The instructions will test you, but never give up. Read each step carefully and take your time. With patience and practice, you'll have these planes streaking across the schoolyard.

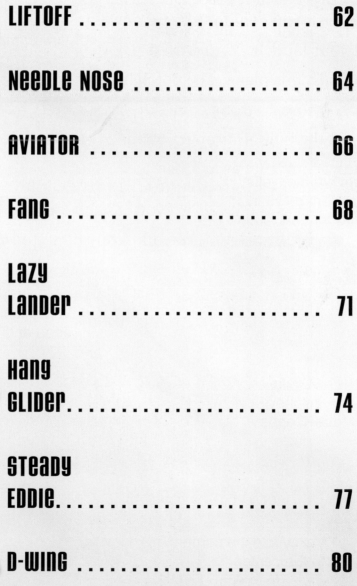

LIFTOFF 62

NEEDLE NOSE 64

AVIATOR 66

FANG 68

LAZY
LANDER 71

HANG
GLIDER 74

STEADY
EDDIE 77

D-WING 80

LIFTOFF

DESIGNED BY CHRISTOPHER L. HARBO

Ever wish you could put more power behind your launch? Your wish is granted with this plane. The notch in Liftoff's nose is strong enough to withstand the pull of a rubber band. Get ready. Aim. Fire away!

Start Here

materials

* 8.5- by 11-inch (22- by 28-centimeter) paper
* scissors
* rubber band

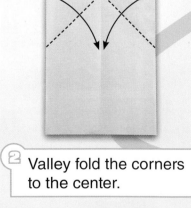

1 Valley fold edge to edge and unfold.

2 Valley fold the corners to the center.

3 Mountain fold the point.

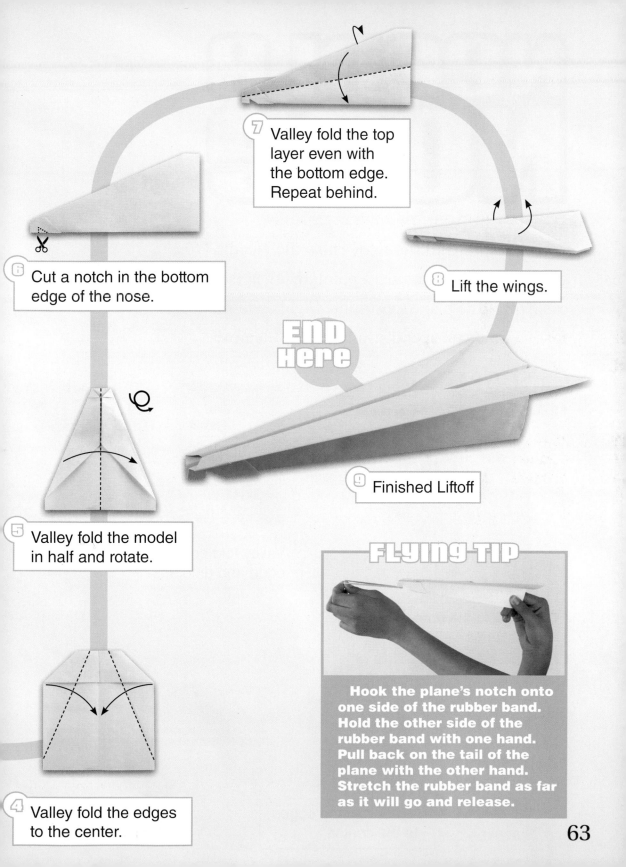

7 Valley fold the top layer even with the bottom edge. Repeat behind.

6 Cut a notch in the bottom edge of the nose.

8 Lift the wings.

END Here

5 Valley fold the model in half and rotate.

9 Finished Liftoff

FLYING TIP

Hook the plane's notch onto one side of the rubber band. Hold the other side of the rubber band with one hand. Pull back on the tail of the plane with the other hand. Stretch the rubber band as far as it will go and release.

4 Valley fold the edges to the center.

63

NEEDLE NOSE

It's not hard to figure out how the Needle Nose got its name. This model's pointy beak gets damaged easily. But the plane's awesome flights will make up for the time you spend straightening the nose.

MATERIALS

• 8.5- by 11-inch (22- by 28-cm) paper

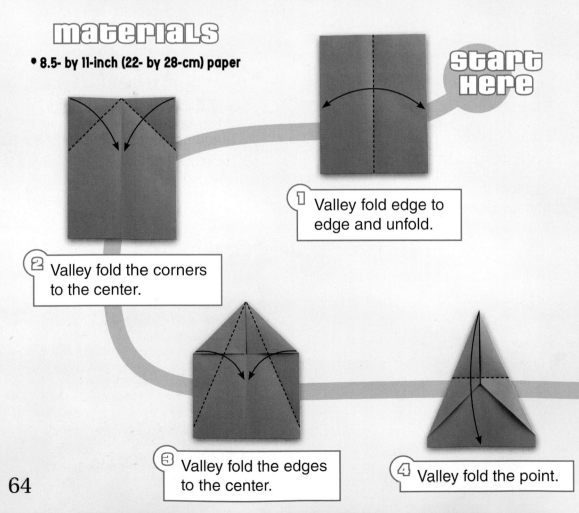

Start Here

1 Valley fold edge to edge and unfold.

2 Valley fold the corners to the center.

3 Valley fold the edges to the center.

4 Valley fold the point.

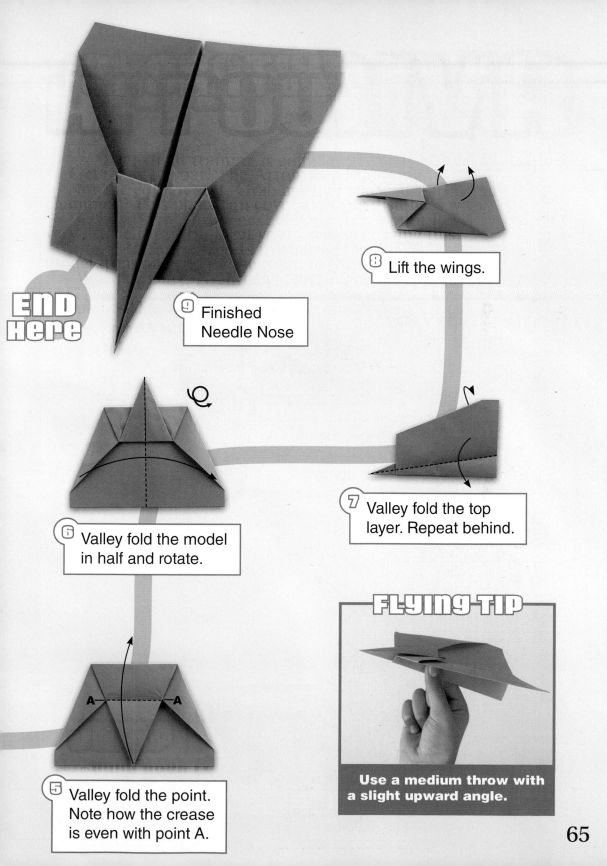

END Here

9 Finished Needle Nose

8 Lift the wings.

7 Valley fold the top layer. Repeat behind.

6 Valley fold the model in half and rotate.

A ──── A

5 Valley fold the point. Note how the crease is even with point A.

FLYING TIP

Use a medium throw with a slight upward angle.

65

AVIATOR

TRADITIONAL MODEL

The Aviator is one cool mini jet. This model looks like a dart and has a built-in cockpit. With a strong throw, you might think a tiny pilot is guiding it across the room.

materials

* 6-inch (15-cm) square of paper

8 Pull up the triangle in the nose to form a cockpit.

9 Lift the wings.

7 Valley fold the top layer even with the bottom edge. Repeat behind.

6 Mountain fold the model in half.

5 Valley fold the edges to the center.

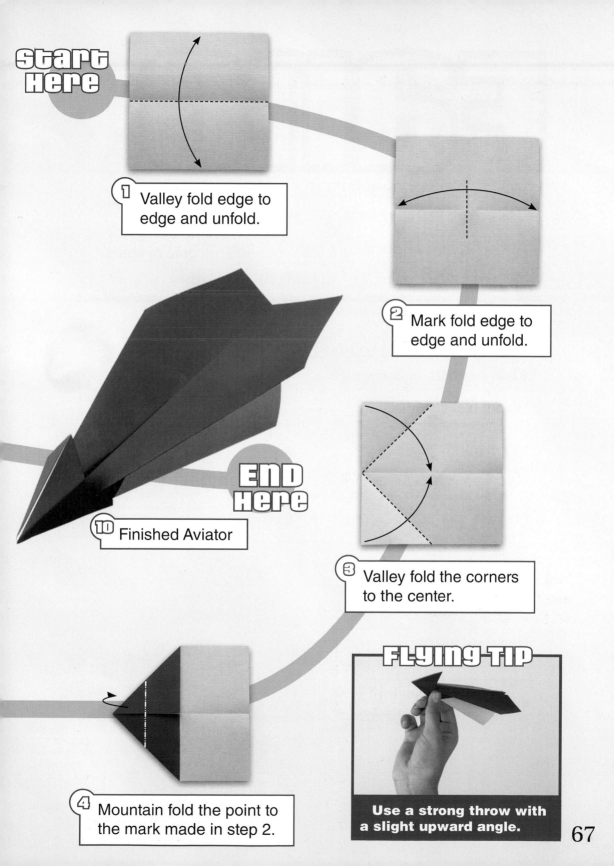

Start Here

1 Valley fold edge to edge and unfold.

2 Mark fold edge to edge and unfold.

3 Valley fold the corners to the center.

END Here

10 Finished Aviator

4 Mountain fold the point to the mark made in step 2.

FLYING TIP

Use a strong throw with a slight upward angle.

67

FANG

DESIGNED BY CHRISTOPHER L. HARBO

Tiny teeth give the Fang a dangerous look, but this gentle glider won't bite. The plane's light wings are at the mercy of air currents. In flight, it sways from side to side as it crosses a room.

materials

* 8.5- by 11-inch (22- by 28-cm) paper

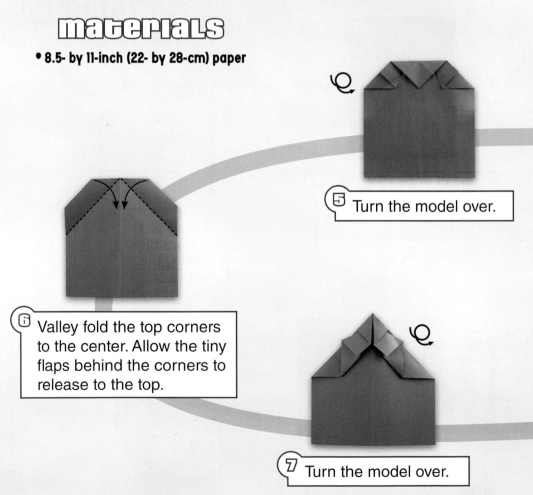

5 Turn the model over.

6 Valley fold the top corners to the center. Allow the tiny flaps behind the corners to release to the top.

7 Turn the model over.

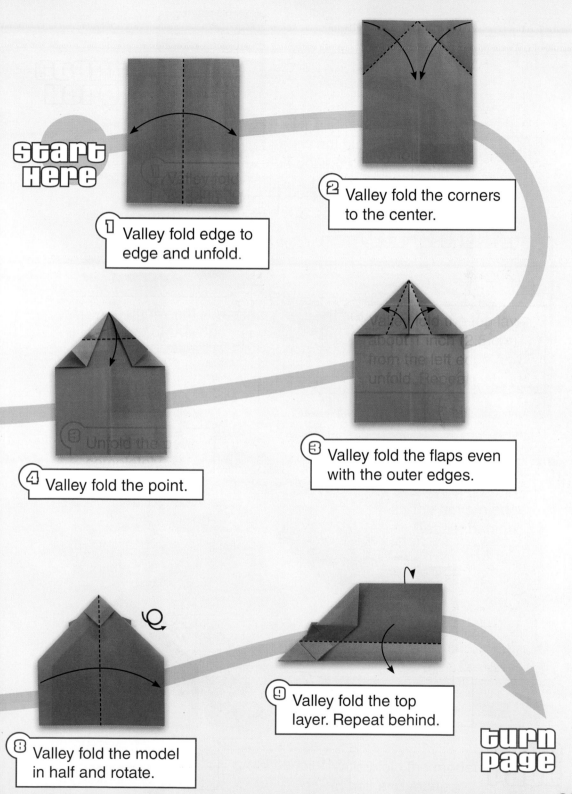

1 Valley fold edge to edge and unfold.

2 Valley fold the corners to the center.

3 Valley fold the flaps even with the outer edges.

4 Valley fold the point.

8 Valley fold the model in half and rotate.

9 Valley fold the top layer. Repeat behind.

Turn Page

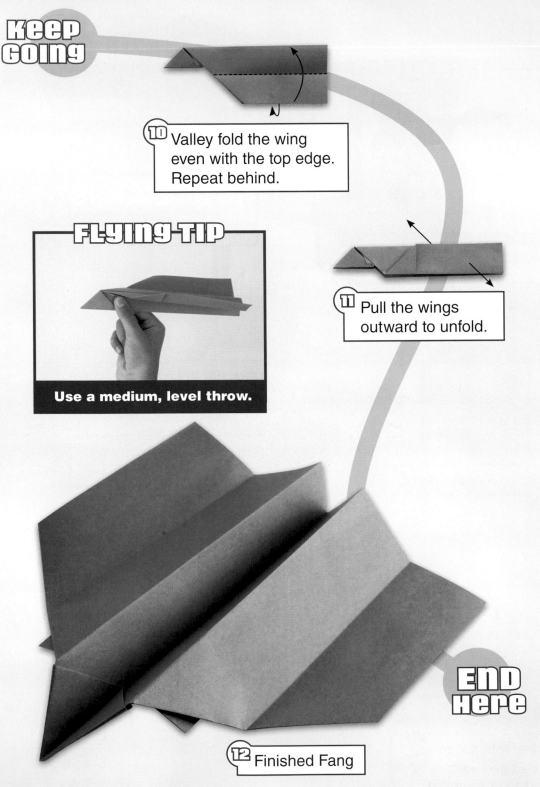

10 Valley fold the wing even with the top edge. Repeat behind.

FLYING TIP

Use a medium, level throw.

11 Pull the wings outward to unfold.

12 Finished Fang

Lazy Lander

DESIGNED BY CHRISTOPHER L. HARBO

Make way for the Lazy Lander! This plane gets its magic from the binder clip. Placed under the nose, the clip gives the glider the weight it needs to fly. Better yet, the clip's legs can serve as landing gear.

materials

* 8.5- by 11-inch (22- by 28-cm) paper
* small binder clip

start here

1 Valley fold edge to edge and unfold.

2 Valley fold the corners to the center.

3 Valley fold the point.

turn page

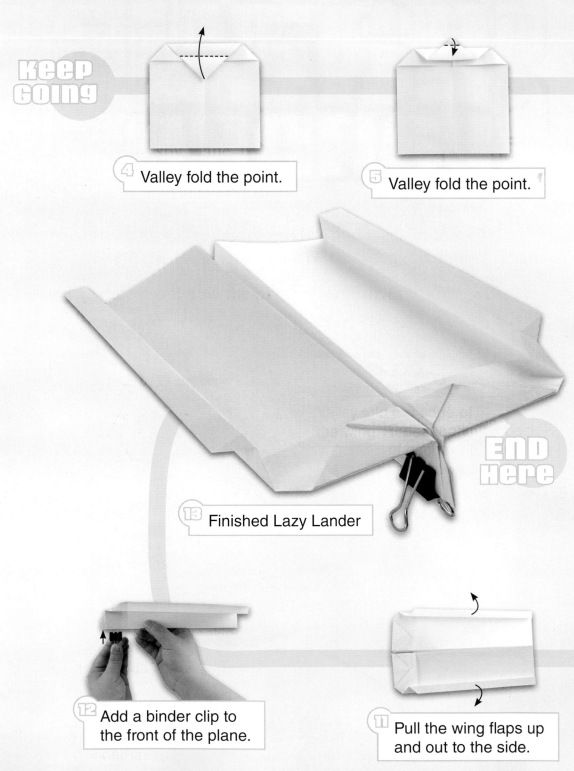

KEEP GOING

4 Valley fold the point.

5 Valley fold the point.

END HERE

13 Finished Lazy Lander

12 Add a binder clip to the front of the plane.

11 Pull the wing flaps up and out to the side.

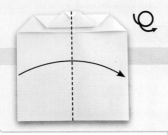

6 Valley fold the model in half and rotate.

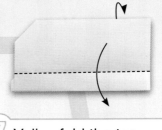

7 Valley fold the top layer. Repeat behind.

FLYING TIP

Use a medium, level throw.

8 Valley fold the edge of the wing. Repeat behind.

10 Lift the wings.

9 Valley fold the wing flap even with the bottom edge. Repeat behind.

73

Hang GLIDER

The Hang Glider takes you soaring to new heights. With the right throw, this glider climbs into the air. When it can go no higher, it banks to the side and curves around the room.

MATERIALS

* **10-inch (25-cm) square of paper**

2 Valley fold to the center and unfold.

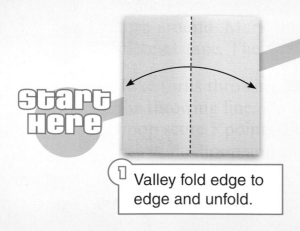

Start Here

1 Valley fold edge to edge and unfold.

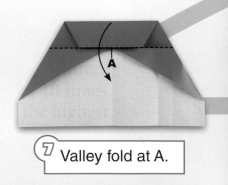

7 Valley fold at A.

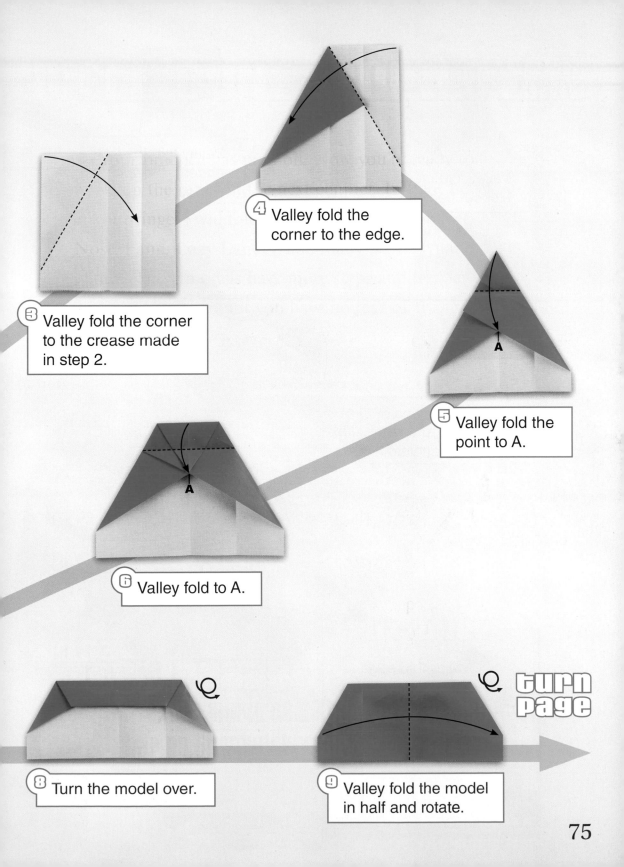

3 Valley fold the corner to the crease made in step 2.

4 Valley fold the corner to the edge.

5 Valley fold the point to A.

A

6 Valley fold to A.

A

8 Turn the model over.

9 Valley fold the model in half and rotate.

turn page

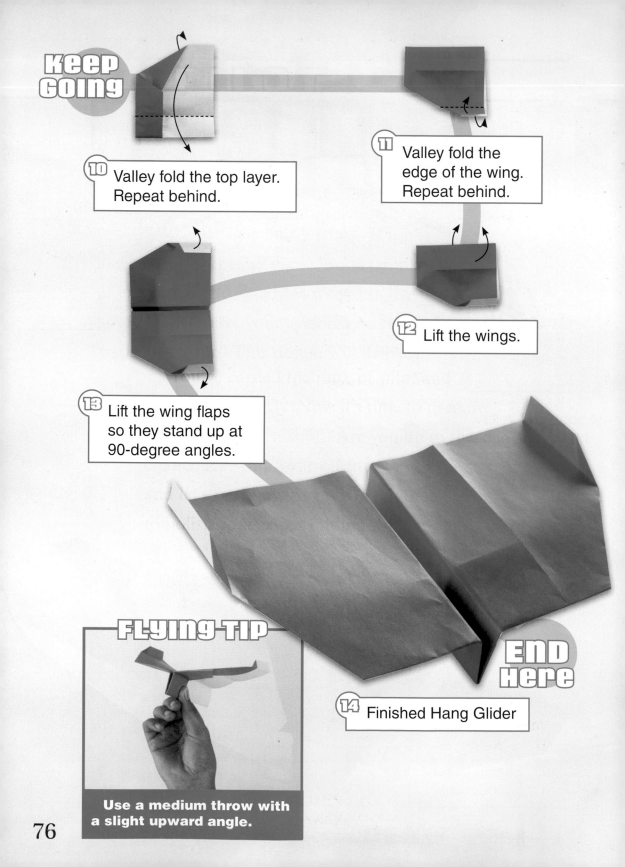

10 Valley fold the top layer. Repeat behind.

11 Valley fold the edge of the wing. Repeat behind.

12 Lift the wings.

13 Lift the wing flaps so they stand up at 90-degree angles.

FLYING TIP

END Here

14 Finished Hang Glider

Use a medium throw with a slight upward angle.

STEADY EDDIE

DESIGNED BY CHRISTOPHER L. HARBO

Get ready for the Steady Eddie. Broad wings and slim wing flaps give this glider a smooth, stable flight. Two small paper clips beside the nose help guide the craft as it comes in for a landing.

materials

* 8.5- by 11-inch (22- by 28-cm) paper
* two small paper clips

start Here

1 Valley fold edge to edge and unfold.

2 Valley fold the corners to the center.

turn page

3 Valley fold the point.

77

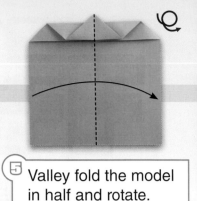

4 Valley fold the point.

5 Valley fold the model in half and rotate.

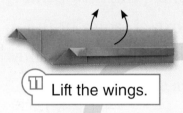

11 Lift the wings.

10 Valley fold the edge of the wing even with the crease made in step 9. Repeat behind.

12 Unfold the wing flaps on the creases made in step 8. Allow the edges of the wings to become L-shaped runners under the wings.

14 Insert a small paper clip on each side of the nose. Turn the model over.

13 Turn the model over.

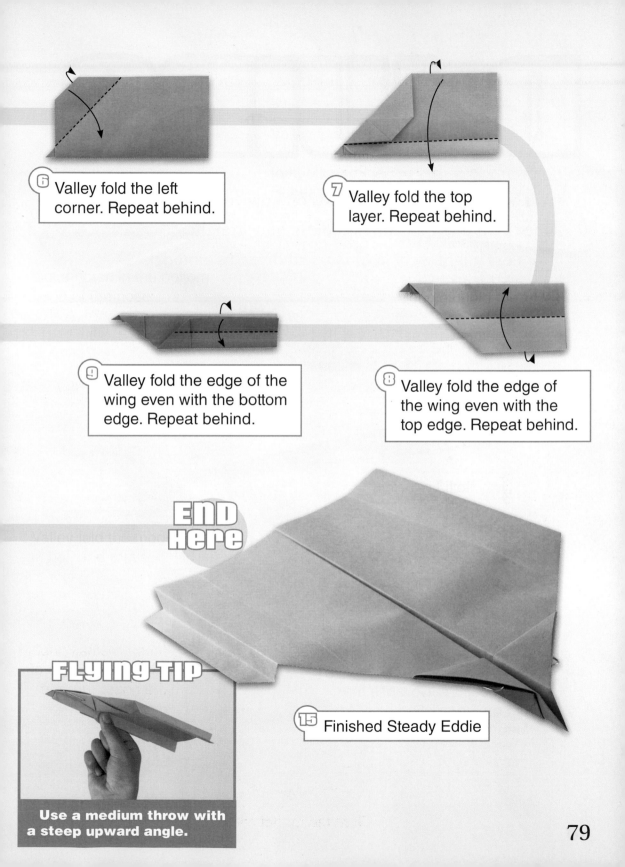

6 Valley fold the left corner. Repeat behind.

7 Valley fold the top layer. Repeat behind.

9 Valley fold the edge of the wing even with the bottom edge. Repeat behind.

8 Valley fold the edge of the wing even with the top edge. Repeat behind.

END HERE

FLYING TIP

15 Finished Steady Eddie

Use a medium throw with a steep upward angle.

D-WING

The D-wing's flight depends on how you release it.
One flight might be long, smooth, and straight.
The next might wobble, curve, and dive. It's a model
that will keep you guessing.

materials

• 8.5- by 11-inch (22- by 28-cm) paper

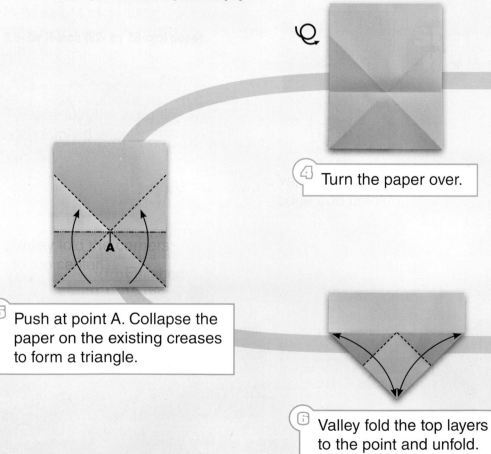

4 Turn the paper over.

5 Push at point A. Collapse the paper on the existing creases to form a triangle.

6 Valley fold the top layers to the point and unfold.

80

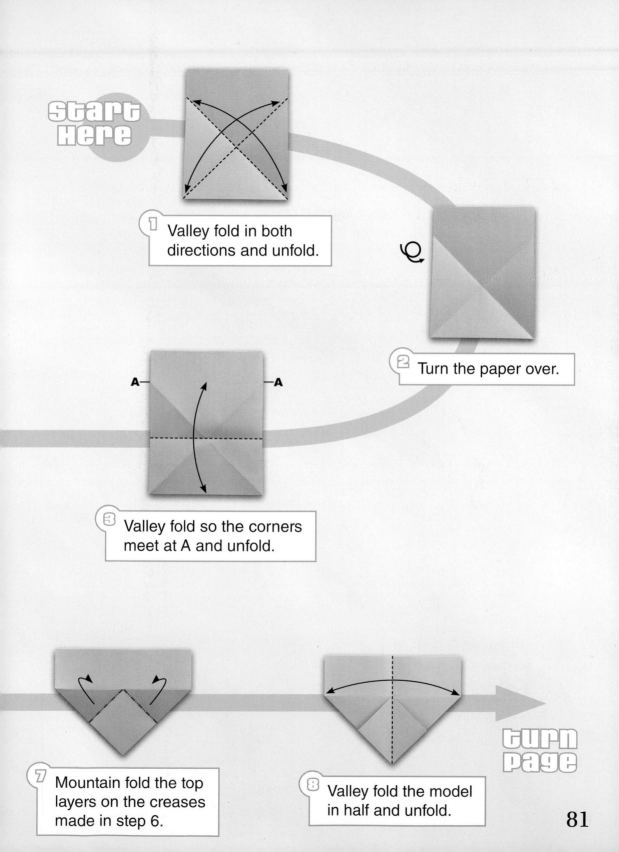

1 Valley fold in both directions and unfold.

2 Turn the paper over.

3 Valley fold so the corners meet at A and unfold.

A—   —A

7 Mountain fold the top layers on the creases made in step 6.

8 Valley fold the model in half and unfold.

turn page

81

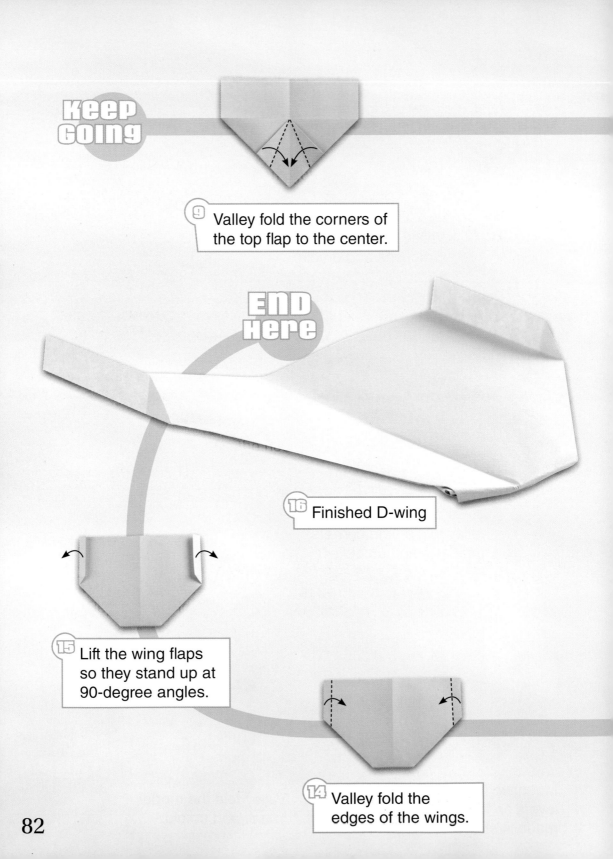

Keep Going

9 Valley fold the corners of the top flap to the center.

End Here

16 Finished D-wing

15 Lift the wing flaps so they stand up at 90-degree angles.

14 Valley fold the edges of the wings.

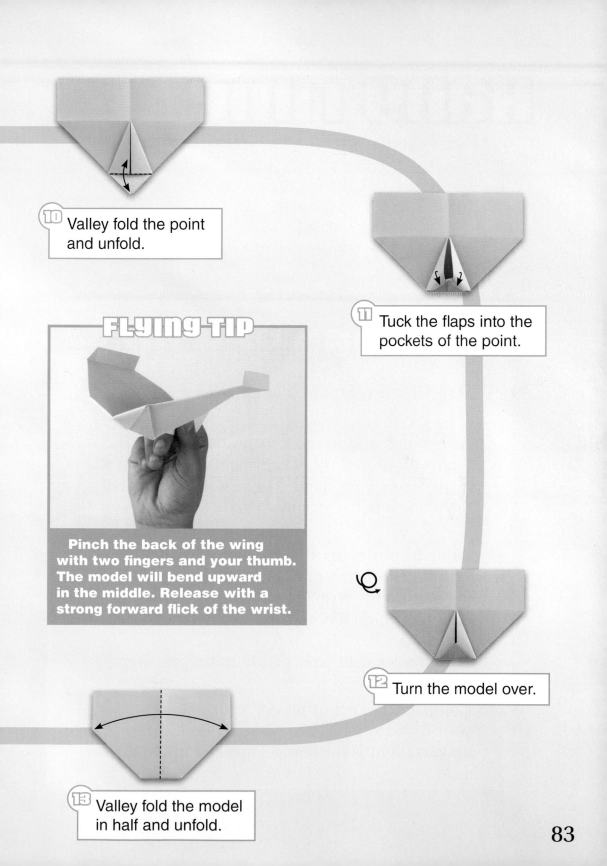

10 Valley fold the point and unfold.

11 Tuck the flaps into the pockets of the point.

FLYING TIP

Pinch the back of the wing with two fingers and your thumb. The model will bend upward in the middle. Release with a strong forward flick of the wrist.

12 Turn the model over.

13 Valley fold the model in half and unfold.

83

Hang Time

How long can you keep a paper airplane in the air? The world record, set by Takuo Toda of Japan, is 27.9 seconds. Challenge a friend to a game of Hang Time to see whose plane can soar the longest.

materials

- large, open room
- stopwatch
- pencil
- notepad
- 2 paper airplanes

WHat you Do

1. Stand in the center of a large, open room.

2. Ask your friend to use a stopwatch to time the flights of your plane. Time begins the instant the plane leaves your hand. Time ends the moment the plane hits the ground.

3. Launch your plane 10 times. Try throwing it with different strengths and angles to achieve the best flight. Write down the flight times for each launch on a notepad.

4. Switch roles with your friend and repeat step 3.

5. Compare the flight times of your plane to your friend's times. The person who has the longest flight is the Hang Time champion.

84

EXCELLENT WORK!

You're an ace paper pilot with nowhere to go but up. Luckily, the next chapter takes you to the highest rank of all. In Captain Level 4, you'll master the Fighter Jet, Warthog, Flying Accordion, and many other incredible planes. These models aren't for the faint of heart. But with the folding skills you've practiced, you should have no trouble at all.

Strap in
and take command of the skies!

You have hours of flight experience under your belt. Now the safety of your passengers and crew rests on your shoulders. The time has come to strap in and take command. As captain, you face the most challenging paper folding.

CONGRATULATIONS ON MAKING THE RANK OF CAPTAIN!

Don't worry if your planes don't look perfect right away. Your first try can be a test plane. Fold the models a second time to make them perfect. Your dedication will soon pay off.

FIGHTER JET 88

WARTHOG 91

GLIDING GRACE 94

FLYING ACCORDION 97

SPACE BOMBER 100

SPARROWHAWK 103

SCREECH OWL 106

FIGHTER JET

TRADITIONAL MODEL

Want a fighter jet that is always ready for its next military mission? This stylish plane swoops through the air. It's a great flier that looks super cool.

MATERIALS

• 6.5- by 11-inch (17- by 28-centimeter) paper

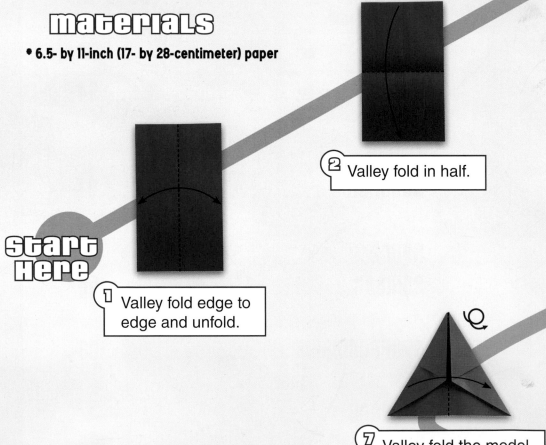

Start Here

1 Valley fold edge to edge and unfold.

2 Valley fold in half.

7 Valley fold the model in half and rotate.

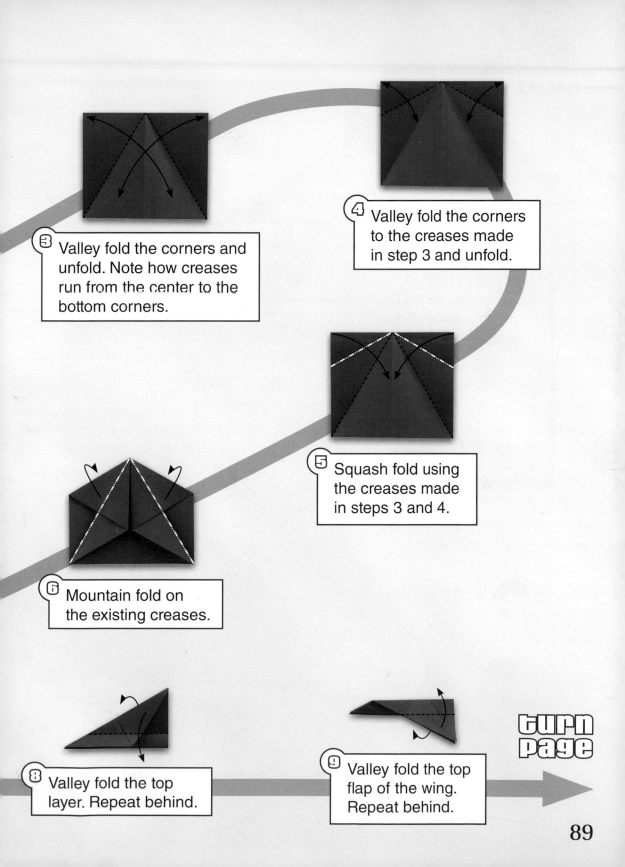

3 Valley fold the corners and unfold. Note how creases run from the center to the bottom corners.

4 Valley fold the corners to the creases made in step 3 and unfold.

5 Squash fold using the creases made in steps 3 and 4.

6 Mountain fold on the existing creases.

8 Valley fold the top layer. Repeat behind.

9 Valley fold the top flap of the wing. Repeat behind.

turn page

89

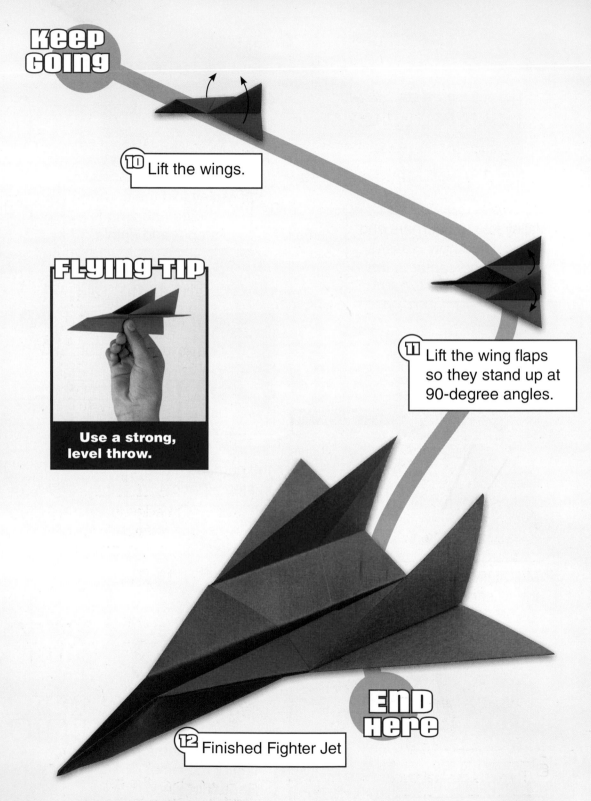

10 Lift the wings.

FLYING TIP

Use a strong, level throw.

11 Lift the wing flaps so they stand up at 90-degree angles.

END HERE

12 Finished Fighter Jet

WARTHOG

DESIGNED BY CHRISTOPHER L. HARBO

The Warthog is a beast. It may not be pretty, but this little glider soars long distances through the air. Don't worry about hitting the wall. The Warthog's snub nose can take a beating.

MATERIALS

- 8.5- by 11-inch (22- by 28-cm) paper

START HERE

1 Valley fold edge to edge and unfold.

2 Valley fold the corners to the center.

3 Turn the model over.

4 Valley fold the edges to the center. Allow the flaps behind to release to the top.

TURN PAGE

91

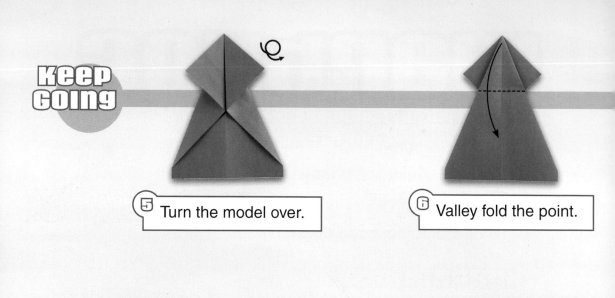

5 Turn the model over.

6 Valley fold the point.

11 Lift the wings.

10 Valley fold the wing flap. Repeat behind.

12 Lift the top layer of the wing flaps and the nose flaps so they stand up at 90-degree angles.

13 Pull the wing flaps outward.

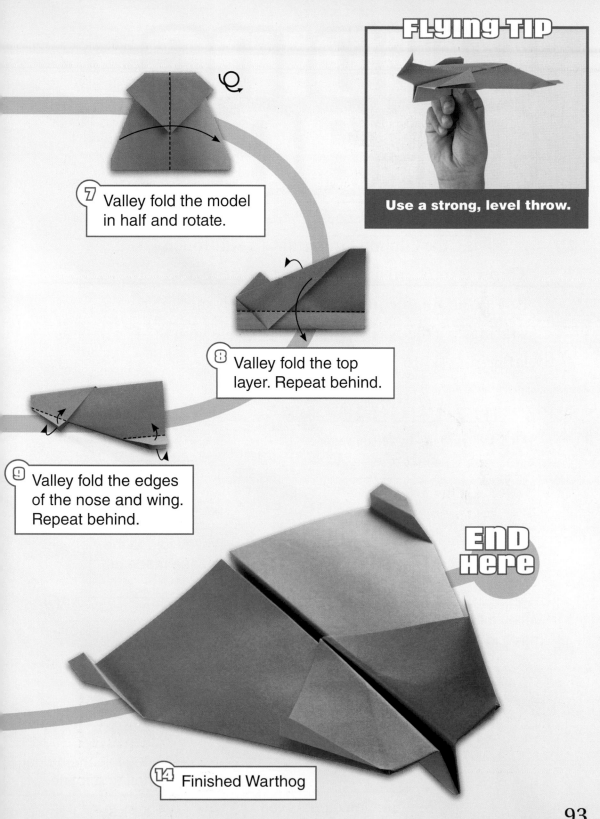

Use a strong, level throw.

7 Valley fold the model in half and rotate.

8 Valley fold the top layer. Repeat behind.

9 Valley fold the edges of the nose and wing. Repeat behind.

END Here

14 Finished Warthog

93

GLIDING Grace

DESIGNED BY CHRISTOPHER L. HARBO

Flying the Gliding Grace takes a soft touch. Throw it too hard and it goes into a steep dive. But a smooth, medium throw sends this model soaring. It's the perfect plane to practice your launching skills.

materials

* 8.5- by 11-inch (22- by 28-cm) paper

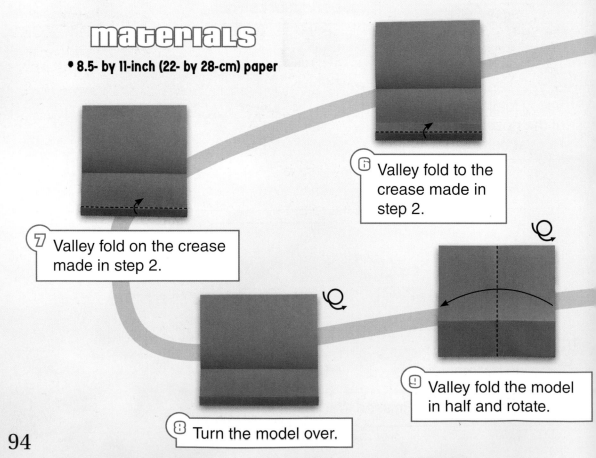

6 Valley fold to the crease made in step 2.

7 Valley fold on the crease made in step 2.

8 Turn the model over.

9 Valley fold the model in half and rotate.

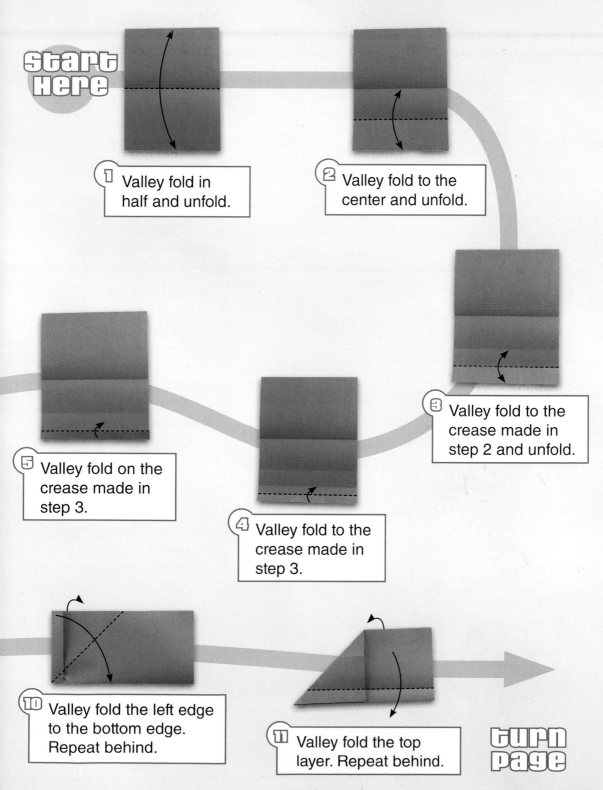

1 Valley fold in half and unfold.

2 Valley fold to the center and unfold.

3 Valley fold to the crease made in step 2 and unfold.

5 Valley fold on the crease made in step 3.

4 Valley fold to the crease made in step 3.

10 Valley fold the left edge to the bottom edge. Repeat behind.

11 Valley fold the top layer. Repeat behind.

turn page

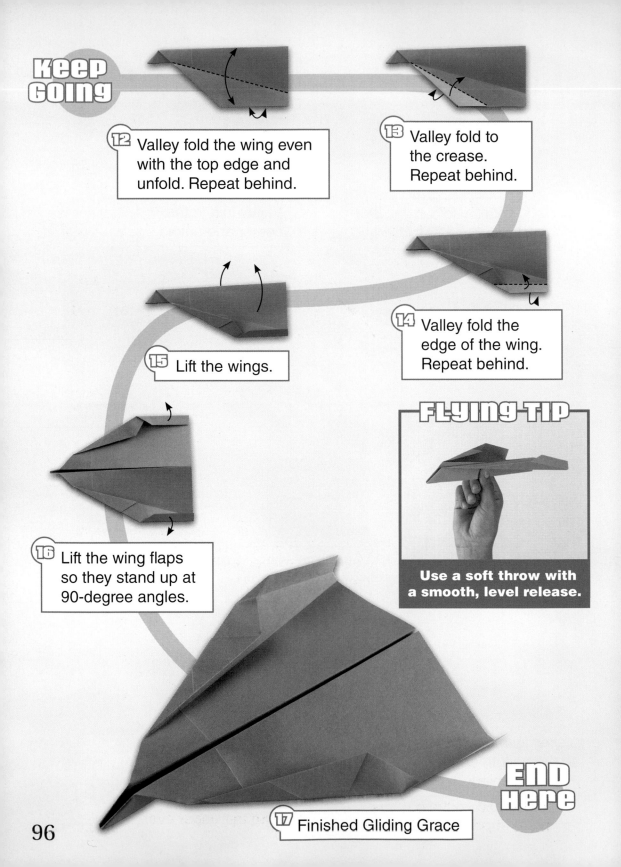

12 Valley fold the wing even with the top edge and unfold. Repeat behind.

13 Valley fold to the crease. Repeat behind.

15 Lift the wings.

14 Valley fold the edge of the wing. Repeat behind.

FLYING TIP

Use a soft throw with a smooth, level release.

16 Lift the wing flaps so they stand up at 90-degree angles.

17 Finished Gliding Grace

END HERE

96

FLYING ACCORDION

Can a paper plane with so many peaks and valleys really fly?
Fold the Flying Accordion and find out. This unique glider will
have your friends begging you to make them one.

materials

* 8.5- by 11-inch (22- by 28-cm) paper

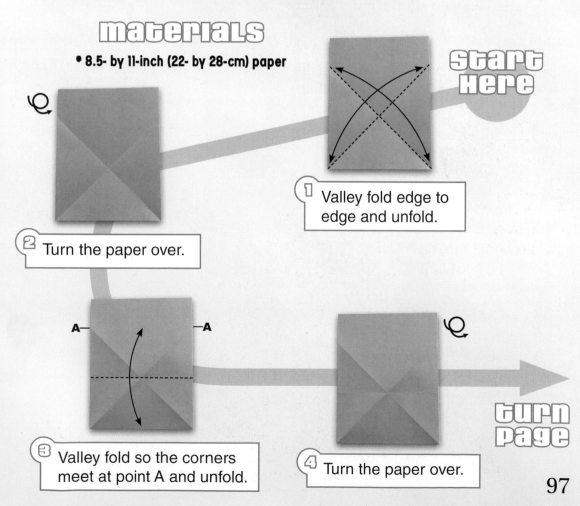

start Here

1 Valley fold edge to edge and unfold.

2 Turn the paper over.

A———A

3 Valley fold so the corners meet at point A and unfold.

4 Turn the paper over.

turn page

97

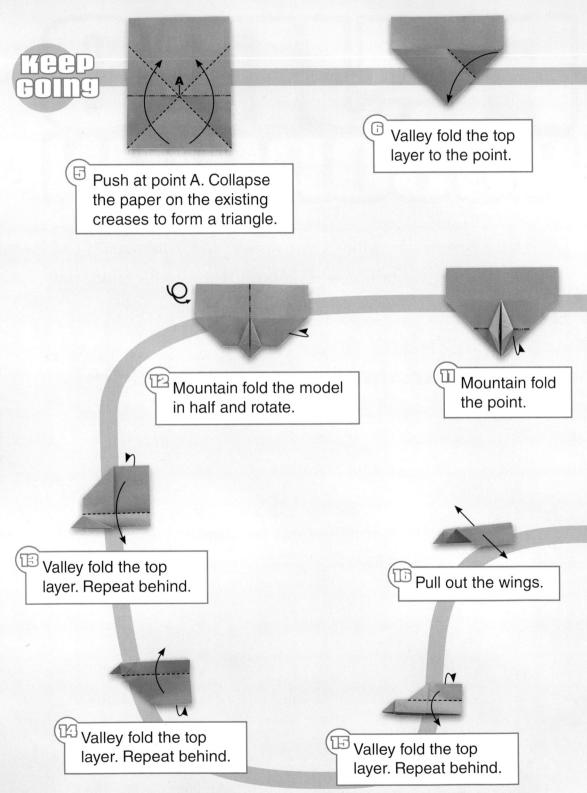

5 Push at point A. Collapse the paper on the existing creases to form a triangle.

6 Valley fold the top layer to the point.

12 Mountain fold the model in half and rotate.

11 Mountain fold the point.

13 Valley fold the top layer. Repeat behind.

16 Pull out the wings.

14 Valley fold the top layer. Repeat behind.

15 Valley fold the top layer. Repeat behind.

7 Valley fold to the center and unfold.

8 Valley fold to the center and unfold.

9 Rabbit ear fold on the creases formed in steps 7 and 8.

10 Repeat steps 6 through 9 on the left side.

END Here

17 Finished Flying Accordion

FLYING TIP

Pinch the plane on the triangle beneath its wings. Give it a medium, level throw.

SPACE BOMBER

TRADITIONAL MODEL

The Space Bomber looks like it flew in from another world. Don't let this plane's boxy shape fool you. Its flight paths are amazingly straight and long.

MATERIALS

* 8.5- by 11-inch (22- by 28-cm) paper

start Here

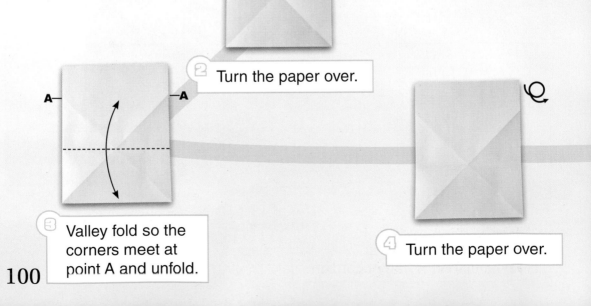

1 Valley fold in both directions and unfold.

2 Turn the paper over.

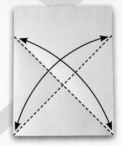

3 Valley fold so the corners meet at point A and unfold.

4 Turn the paper over.

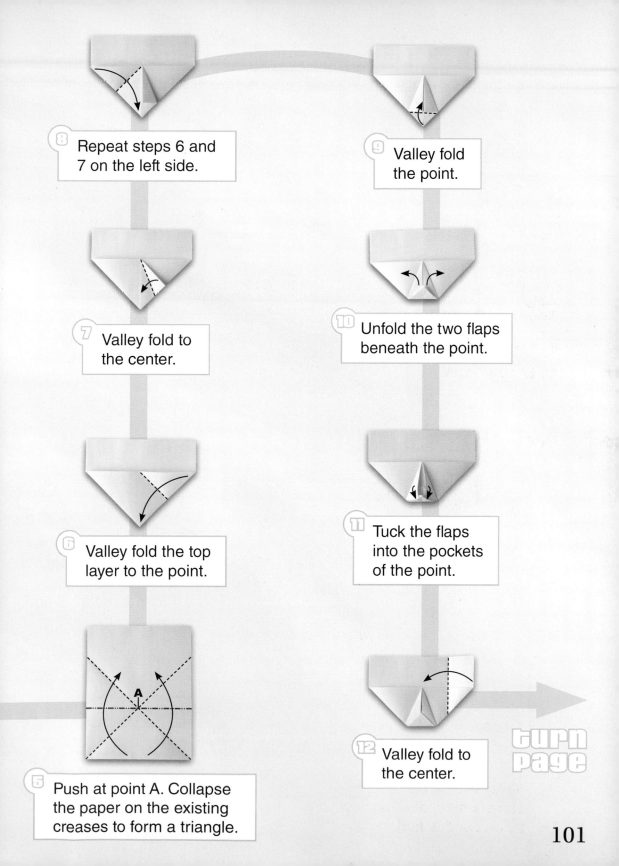

8 Repeat steps 6 and 7 on the left side.

9 Valley fold the point.

7 Valley fold to the center.

10 Unfold the two flaps beneath the point.

6 Valley fold the top layer to the point.

11 Tuck the flaps into the pockets of the point.

5 Push at point A. Collapse the paper on the existing creases to form a triangle.

12 Valley fold to the center.

turn page

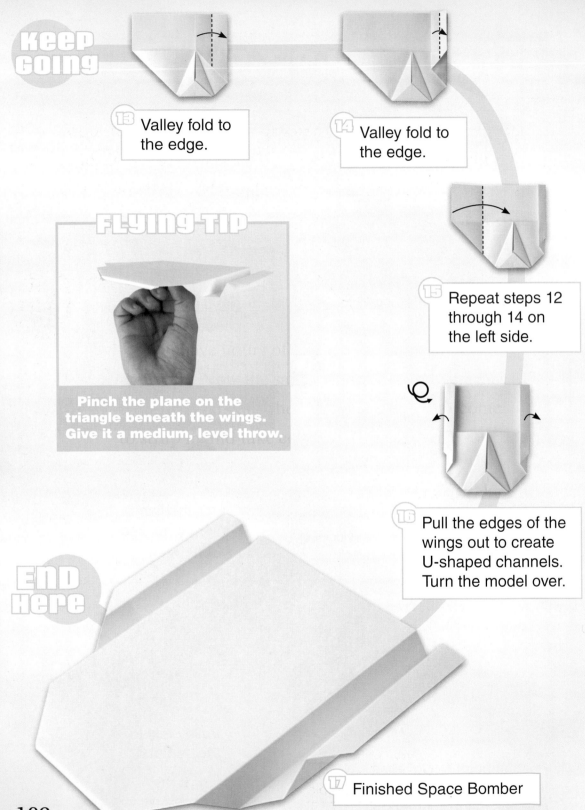

13 Valley fold to the edge.

14 Valley fold to the edge.

FLYING TIP

Pinch the plane on the triangle beneath the wings. Give it a medium, level throw.

15 Repeat steps 12 through 14 on the left side.

16 Pull the edges of the wings out to create U-shaped channels. Turn the model over.

END HERE

17 Finished Space Bomber

102

Sparrowhawk

Traditional model

Do you want the Sparrowhawk to sail like a glider or loop around like a stunt plane? Changing the power and angle of your throw will determine how this plane flies. Either way, the Sparrowhawk doesn't disappoint.

materials

* 8.5- by 11-inch (22- by 28-cm) paper

start Here

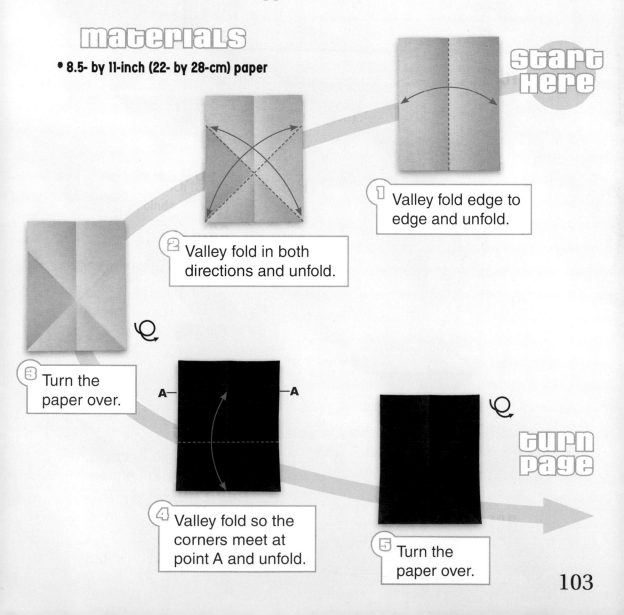

1 Valley fold edge to edge and unfold.

2 Valley fold in both directions and unfold.

3 Turn the paper over.

A — — — A

4 Valley fold so the corners meet at point A and unfold.

5 Turn the paper over.

turn page

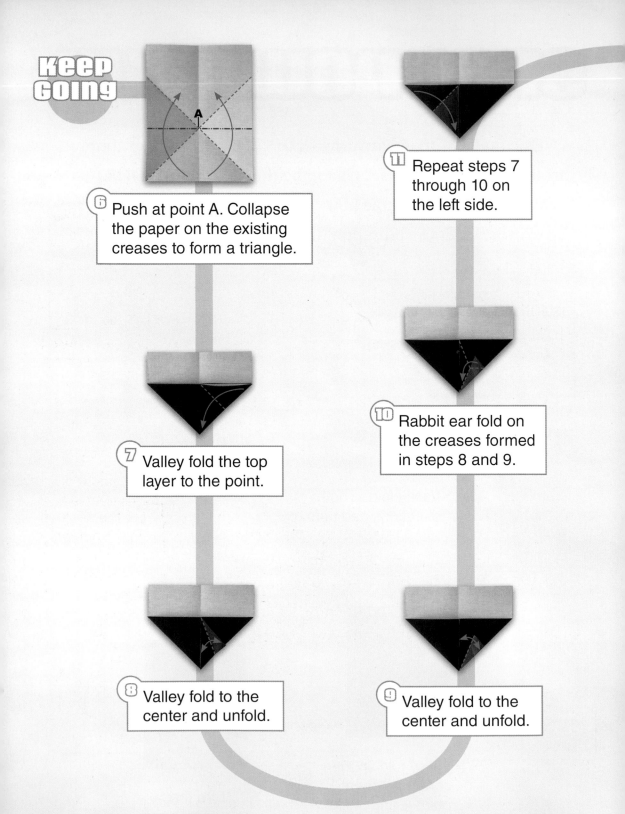

6 Push at point A. Collapse the paper on the existing creases to form a triangle.

7 Valley fold the top layer to the point.

8 Valley fold to the center and unfold.

11 Repeat steps 7 through 10 on the left side.

10 Rabbit ear fold on the creases formed in steps 8 and 9.

9 Valley fold to the center and unfold.

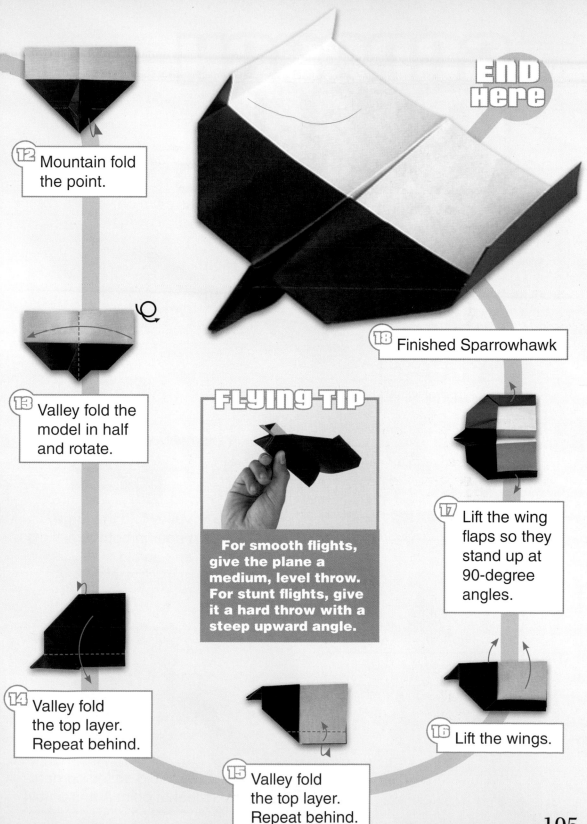

12 Mountain fold the point.

13 Valley fold the model in half and rotate.

14 Valley fold the top layer. Repeat behind.

15 Valley fold the top layer. Repeat behind.

16 Lift the wings.

17 Lift the wing flaps so they stand up at 90-degree angles.

18 Finished Sparrowhawk

END HERE

FLYING TIP

For smooth flights, give the plane a medium, level throw. For stunt flights, give it a hard throw with a steep upward angle.

screech OWL

TRADITIONAL MODEL

With its wide wings and narrow tail, the Screech Owl glides like a silent hunter. Hold it as high as you can to get the longest flight.

materials

* 7- by 10.5-inch (18- by 27-cm) paper
* scissors

4 Valley fold the large paper in both directions and unfold.

5 Turn the paper over.

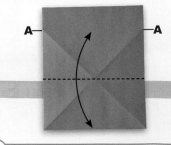

A————————A

6 Valley fold so the corners meet at point A and unfold.

106

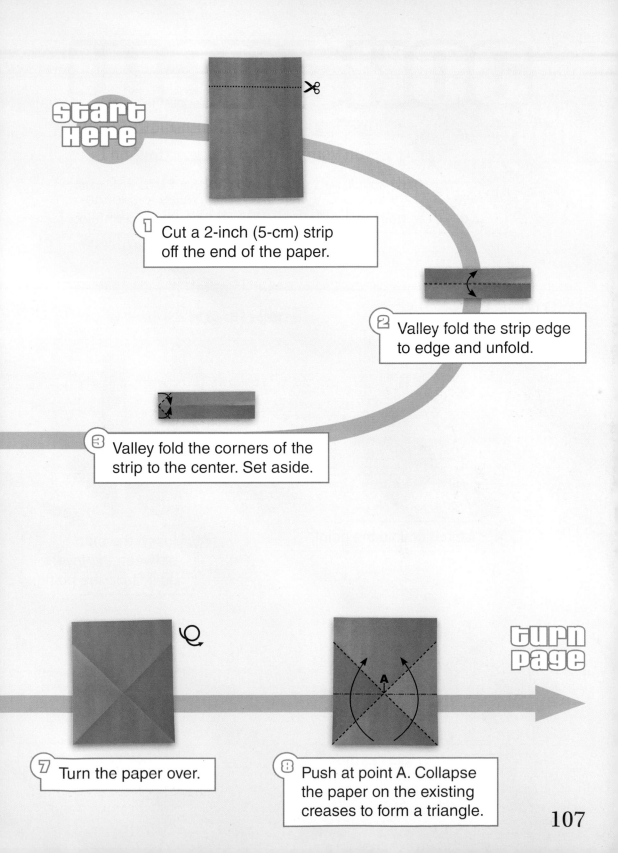

1   Cut a 2-inch (5-cm) strip off the end of the paper.

2   Valley fold the strip edge to edge and unfold.

3   Valley fold the corners of the strip to the center. Set aside.

turn page

7   Turn the paper over.

8   Push at point A. Collapse the paper on the existing creases to form a triangle.

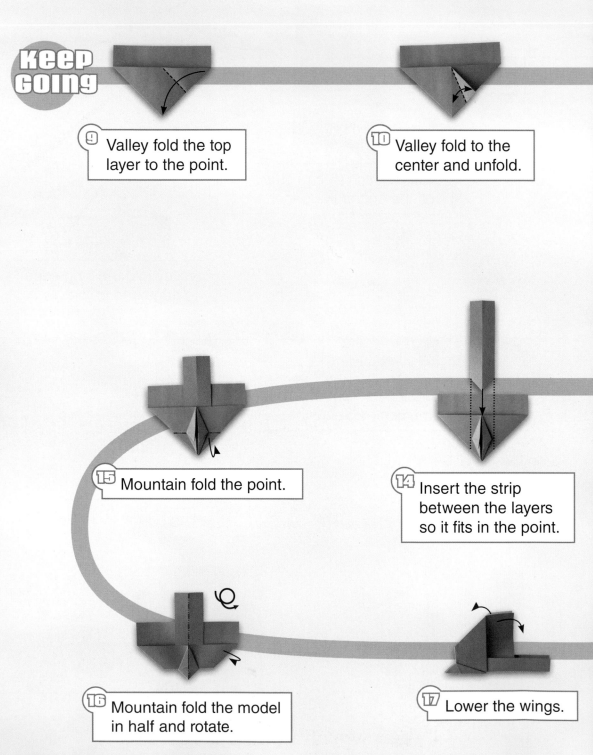

9 Valley fold the top layer to the point.

10 Valley fold to the center and unfold.

15 Mountain fold the point.

14 Insert the strip between the layers so it fits in the point.

16 Mountain fold the model in half and rotate.

17 Lower the wings.

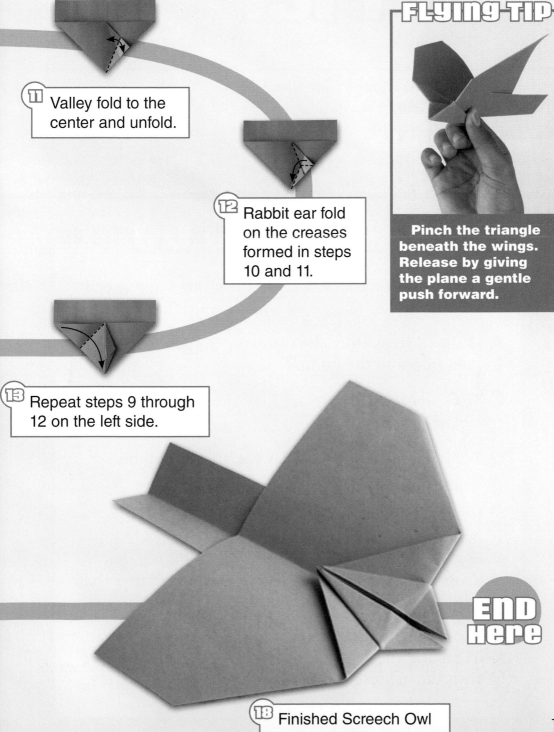

11 Valley fold to the center and unfold.

12 Rabbit ear fold on the creases formed in steps 10 and 11.

Pinch the triangle beneath the wings. Release by giving the plane a gentle push forward.

13 Repeat steps 9 through 12 on the left side.

END Here

18 Finished Screech Owl

109

Aircraft Carrier

Fighter pilots use incredible skill to land their speeding jets on aircraft carrier decks. Here's your chance to test your landing skills. Challenge a friend to a game of Aircraft Carrier.

materials

- rope
- 3 hula hoops
- 2 paper airplanes
- pencil
- notepad

WHat you DO

1. Place a short piece of rope on the ground at one end of your yard or playground. This is your throwing line.

2. Walk 10 steps from the throwing line and lay one hula hoop on the ground.

3. Walk another 10 steps and lay the second hoop on the ground.

4. Walk 10 more steps and lay the third hoop on the ground.

5. Return to the throwing line and take turns launching planes toward the hoops. Planes that land in the first hoop score 3 points. Planes that drop in the middle hoop score 5 points. Planes that land in the farthest hoop score 10 points.

6. Write down the scores of each flight on a notepad. Then add the scores for each player. The player with the highest score is the champion.

OUTSTANDING JOB!

You've conquered *The Ultimate Guide to Paper Airplanes*. Now you know how to fold and fly 35 unique paper gliders. But with your well-honed skills, why stop here? Visit your local library and check out other books on paper airplanes. You'll find dozens of models you've never seen before. And if you're feeling really adventurous, try creating a few paper planes of your own.

YOU MAY BE SURPRISED
when your own ideas take flight!

The Ultimate Guide to Paper Airplanes is published by Capstone Press,
1710 Roe Crest Drive, North Mankato, Minnesota 56003.
www.capstonepub.com

Library of Congress Cataloging-in-Publication Data
Harbo, Christopher L.
 The ultimate guide to paper airplanes : 35 amazing step-by-step
designs! / by Christopher L. Harbo.
    p. cm—(Edge books; Paper Airplanes)
 ISBN 978-1-4296-5648-1 (bind up)
 1. Paper airplanes—Juvenile literature. I. Title. II. Series.
 TL778.H3736 2010
 745.592—dc22   2010026489

Editorial Credits
Kyle Grenz, designer; Marcie Spence, media researcher; Marcy Morin, scheduler;
    Laura Manthe, production specialist

Photo Credits
Capstone Studio/Karon Dubke, all planes and steps
Shutterstock/newphotoservice, cover (background); Serg64, cover (background)

Printed in China
5070